7 SECRETS OF BUILDING ELITE SALESTEAMS

Proven Ways to Increase Sales Results For Sales Managers and Sales Executives

DIANE POLNOW

Published By Elite Sales Leaders
10 9 8 7 6 5 4 3 2 1

Cover Design: Dawn Teagarden
Interior Design: Dawn Teagarden

7 Secrets of Building Elite Sales Teams
Copyright © 2016
First Edition
ISBN# 978-0-9882999-1-7
258 pages

1) Management
2) Executive Development
3) Leadership Development
4) Sales

Printed in the United States of America

Cataloging-in-Publication Data Available Upon Request

For more information contact:
Diane Polnow
Email: Diane@EliteSalesLeaders.com
Phone: 1.310.421.5271
www.EliteSalesLeaders.com
www.DianePolnow.com

DEDICATION

To my dad for instilling in me a rock solid work ethic, strong morals, and high values. For a man of few words, I heard you even when you weren't speaking.

To my mom for being a working mom, for being tough on me so I was better prepared for the business world, and for showing me that a woman can work *and* thrive.

To everyone I've managed, thank you for helping me grow. I've learned so much from each of you over the years and am honored to have you as friends. My wish is that you would have everything you want in your life. And I also wish you incredible success in all you do.

To all those who have managed me, thank you for all you've taught me and for your patience and guidance. I learned so much from you (and yes, I know I wasn't always easy to manage).

To all those managers and leaders who never really had anyone help guide or manage them. May I have a positive impact on your career and may you have the unlimited amount of success you deserve.

DIANE POLNOW

is the Ideal ROI Consultant, Coach, Trainer, and Mentor for You and Your Company

Hire Diane for your next: Corporate Event, Sales Meeting, Seminar, Coaching Program, or Sales Training

FOR BOOKING:

Call: 1-310-421-5271

Email: Info@EliteSalesLeaders.com

www.EliteSalesLeaders.com

www.DianePolnow.com

PRAISE FROM ELITE SALES LEADERS

"There's a reason Diane has been a Top Performer in some of the largest Fortune 500 companies. She knows her business, she knows the psychology of people, and she knows how to get results. She'll give you more than your money's worth. Her work is priceless."

—Christine Adzich, Former Senior Manager, Gartner Group

"Diane was my Sales Manager for six years at Sprint. During the time I worked for Diane, she brought many incredible assets, skills and support to our team. I was consistently one of the top salespeople in the area, and I did not accomplish this alone. Diane's strength in building a winning team is in knowing where people are best suited. She has great emotional intelligence and high ethical standards. The fundamental aspects of Diane's approach and management style encouraged the following: Inspired me to do my personal best, helped remove internal and external roadblocks, constantly made herself available to discuss concerns, encouraged creative solutions, and fostered a fun, hardworking, winning team. Diane is truly a unique and wonderful person. I was very fortunate to work for her. In the ten years I worked for Sprint, the last six years working for her were the best!"

—Elizabeth Black, former Corporate Account Executive, Sprint

"I have collaborated on many projects with Diane personally and find her insight, knowledge and relational skills truly amazing. She is able to delicately capture the deeper needs of her peers/clients to help them create profitable and sustainable business decisions. She is meticulous in her attention to detail and maintaining rapport with all she comes in contact with."

—Liz Marushin, Former Time Warner Cable, Management/Executive Trainer

"Working with Diane has always been an uplifting experience. Her enthusiasm and for getting things done and her insight into how to work together to accomplish projects or goals is contagious, inspiring and energizing. You can't resist her can do approach!"

—Ramona Yoh, Protection One, Commercial Sales Consultant

"I have had the privilege to see and experience Diane's sales expertise and management style up close. If you want to build an Elite sales force, then I wholeheartedly urge you to contact Diane. She possesses a remarkable blend of experience and character that will lead you and your teams to success."

—Matt Patterson, Founder/President, Matt Patterson International

"Diane Polnow is a class act. She is polished and professional but also extremely fun and personable. She has a way of quickly creating trusting relationships by being an incredible listener. She makes your goals, her goals. The sales team principles and systems that Diane has created are unique and effective. I recommend Diane's services without hesitation!"

—LeAnn Fritz, ND, CNHP, New Hope Health

"Diane is simply amazing. She is patient, hard working, and one of a kind. I have loved working with her and would give her the highest recommendation"

—Ryan Krane, Ryan Krane Training Method

"Diane Polnow is truly an inspiring leader! She maintains her authenticity and reveals her humanity, creating trust and connection with her people. With her depth of knowledge and coaching style, she leads her teams to be Top Performers in sales on a consistent basis."

—Jani Ashmore, Author, *Stop Managing Start Inspiring: Keys for Leaders to Bring Out the Best in Others*

Here are some high-profile clients Diane has worked with throughout her corporate career:

Toyota

Fox

Sony

Boeing

Tenet Healthcare

Disney

Marriott

Time Warner Cable

Fresh 'N Easy

Universal Studios

CONTENTS

INTRODUCTION

WELCOME TO A WORLD OF UNIQUE OPPORTUNITY

IF I COULD SHOW you how to become part of an elite group of people who **make more money, experience higher job satisfaction, and have priceless skill sets** that you can use for the rest of your career, would you be interested? Great—because that's what I plan to do. During my long and successful career in sales and sales management, I discovered and utilized some of the best-kept secrets for sales success in the corporate arena. Now I'll share with you the

> **Elite:** noun, adjective
> A group of people considered by others or themselves to be the best in a particular society or category, esp. because of their power, talent, or wealth. As in "the wealthy, educated elite." Synonyms: best, crème de la crème, elect, high society, jet set, beautiful people, beau monde, haut monde, glitterati, aristocracy.

strategies I used throughout my career that allowed me to consistently post high performance and stay at the top of the ranking report year after year.

Why This Book Needed to Exist

When it comes to finding and keeping great sales talent, encouraging teams to collaborate in order to accelerate results, and motivating salespeople to push harder for the rewards they are ultimately working for in life, the corporate world faces a fundamental problem. The issue is not that times have changed. We all know that the world of business is rapidly changing. No, the real problem is this:

Management styles have not changed with the times.

I'm always shocked to witness that even today, when salespeople aren't performing, managers seem to automatically default to micromanagement. It's amazing this practice still exists in an age where personal independence and the ability to choose our own paths is propagated through every possible medium, including the vast expanses of our social networks.

The old ways of short-leash management no longer suffice. I'm confident that no one on Earth enjoys being micromanaged. I don't. Today, it's about collaboration rather than coercion, and positive reinforcement rather than fear tactics. I'm also confident that none of the people who work with you—notice I said work *with* you, not *for* you—want to be micromanaged. That's why I have always taught my teams and now my clients the most updated management techniques that are proven to help you stay the leader of the charts. That means you'll be making the income you want and your job will actually be much more fun and less stressful. It's time for a brain overhaul—time to stop perpetuating an attitude of, "I'm your manager. You work FOR me." A new, more powerful and effective mindset is:

"I'm here to work with you, to help you, and to serve."

The old ways of managing are still the ones being encouraged. What's most frustrating is that there seems to be endless material readily available on the market on *how to sell*, but the critical missing piece is on *how to manage*. That's a significant problem. If top salespeople aren't managed properly, they'll leave to go be a top producer for someone else. That's why I knew that somewhere out there had to exist a better way to manage, a better way to lead, and a better way to encourage your team to reach their fullest potential and become top performers. The techniques I learned throughout my career became the solution to this problem.

My Journey to the Solution

A career in sales is daunting enough, let alone sales management. It's certainly not for everyone. Many can't fathom the thought of working and thriving in the world of sales or the world of managing others. For some, the thought of working in corporate makes them panic; for others, it's their golden ticket...a dream come true.

For me, it was something I was taught to embrace by my parents. They instilled in me the belief that the road to happiness, career satisfaction, and financial stability entailed graduating from high school with good grades, graduating from college with good grades, finding a job with a good company, and working there for the rest of my life. For that reason, I grew up with the ultimate goal of getting the right education and then being hired by an established, respected company.

That's what I did. My first job after college was with Kroy Lettering Systems. I was required to dress in a suit, only to sit inside a bleak, grey cubicle with a telephone attached to my hand. It was the quintessential inside telemarketing job, filled with elation when a client said *yes*, coupled with anxiety as our boss paced over us like a hungry lion, listening to every word—judging, scoring, and critiquing. That was my first real experience with being micromanaged. I quickly recognized that it wasn't the environment for me.

I knew it was time to move on to something bigger and better. I landed my next job with Philip Morris, the GIANT of big companies. I went from making telephone calls in a windowless cube to driving a new company car through a beautiful sales territory, working for a fantastic boss, getting generous pay, and best of all, having freedom. No more stifling grey walls. I finally got a glimpse of what it was like to sell in the Big Leagues, and if this was what it was like, then I was all in.

"Put me in coach. I'm ready to play!"

Well, I *was* ready to get into the game until I started getting called the "Cigarette Girl." I loved working for Philip Morris, but I recognized that their image did not fit my own personal brand. I knew it was time to move on and find a new label and a new brand that fit with the persona I envisioned for myself.

A dear friend, also named Diane, and myself decided we couldn't stay another day in the blistering Arizona heat, so we packed our bags and moved to Beverly. It wasn't Beverly *Hills*, but it was California—the land of opportunity. We rented a U-Haul and drove across the desert headed for… no job and no place to live. Our only backup plan was to move back to Arizona if we didn't like it. (We're both still here.)

Our bright eyes and grand ideas of success led to us to pursue careers in the booming California real estate market. One day during a round of golf, I met a successful real estate investor from Australia who sent me to interview for my next job. Soon after, I started working for a small builder who sold $3 million to $4 million ocean view homes with elevators. It was a sweet gig.

After the development sold out, I managed to land a top job as the third sales manager at Sprint PCS in the brand new wireless division. I was a consistent Top Performing Manager and was soon promoted to start their new National Accounts division. I thrived year-after-year, being consistently ranked as a Top Sales Manager, achieved multiple President's Club awards, and survived multiple reorganizations as well as an extremely challenging company merger.

Then, after fourteen years, I accepted a position with American Express, one the of the Top 100 companies to work for according to Fortune.com.[1] I inherited a team that ranked #33 in the nation and guided them to the #10 spot in less than two years, then on to the #4 ranking by January our third year. It was clear to everyone who worked with me that I had discovered how to get my teams and myself on the fast track to sales success and stay there. My forte and brand was that I could flip low performing salespeople and teams to Top Performing salespeople and teams.

Some Surprising Reflections

Corporate America has provided me with great training, an amazing skill set, and the ability to speak and understand

1 http://fortune.com/best-companies/

corporate language, as well as an adept knowledge of the entire sales process and organizational structure. It has also blessed me with a 401K, amazing benefits, and the best office view of all—the view from a virtual office. I had truly thrived through the help of some phenomenal teachers over the years and through my own ambition and willingness to think outside the traditional manager's box.

As I began to reflect on that journey, I wondered where I got my drive. I was surprised by the answer. I recognized that much of my hustle and ambition came from years of my mother telling me I wasn't good enough. When I was growing up, she would tell me that she didn't care for my hairstyle, my clothes, or my makeup. She was the archetypal "criticizing mother". I could never *do* enough, *be* enough, or do it *well* enough, despite the fact that I was an honor roll student, captain of the cheer squad and pompom squad, on student counsel, and held down a job throughout high school.

I knew my mother loved me and, in her own mind, she probably thought she was pushing me to become better. In a sense, she was. Her methods were harsh by most people's standards, but they did push me to excel. In fact, I excelled at just about everything. The problem was I didn't see it. I didn't feel it. I didn't celebrate it. Whenever I would succeed or win some award, I just kept my head down and pushed even harder as I thought: "No, that's not good enough. Keep going."

In hindsight, which is much clearer than 20/20, I know this mentality is what caused me to stay too long in some positions. It also caused me to be okay with not receiving the acknowledgement or recognition I deserved from others. I just didn't realize that the right management would have encouraged me to keep rising and would have helped me recognize and celebrate my own strengths a little sooner.

I also realized that my mother's micromanagement style and critical approach closely mirrored the way that many managers still handle their salespeople. So, I'm grateful for every step of the way, because I learned so much about what *not* to do.

All those years of seeing how *not* to manage others is what makes me so passionate about helping others learn how to drive Elite performance.

Because of those experiences, I now have the knowledge and capability to help you become an Elite Sales Leader, saving you years of learning and countless hours of frustration.

Buckle In

As times change, so should our management techniques. Too few managers today are trained to manage *people*. They're taught products and services, but not up-to-date, positive management skills that drive Top Performance. Most importantly, they are not taught how to treat their people.

I want to help you learn to manage in fresh, effective ways so you can climb to the top and stay there.

In the old school model of management, you wouldn't dare share your secrets if you were on to something that gave you big results. You'd keep that technique hidden to maintain your edge. Today, sharing and collaborating are what helps drive peak performance. There's enough bounty out there for all of us, so I encourage you to raise the bar with me and help everyone thrive. You can enjoy a career and a life full of *abundance* by using the same skills that I used to climb to the top in Corporate America.

This book is filled with my no-fluff, real world, proven principles that you can easily duplicate. If implemented properly and consistently, they will help you and your sales teams rise quickly to the top of the heap. I am sharing them with you so you can achieve peak results, make more money, increase job satisfaction, lower employee turnover, and prove that having a heart in business *does* work and *can* drive results.

This is not a motivational book or a self-help guide, although I hope you feel both motivated and helped when you are finished. Those types of books are important to your overall success, but you can find countless works on motivation, leadership, and selling. What's missing on the bookshelves is how to manage a diverse group of personalities in order to drive stellar performance and consistent top results. That's why this book is designed with one targeted objective in mind: To help YOU stand out in today's business world as a superstar and as an exemplary sales leader.

So let's jump in and get to the bottom line… FAST.

SECRET 1

IT'S ALL ABOUT THE COACH

WANTED: A RADICAL SHIFT IN LEADERSHIP MENTALITY

"Practice Golden Rule #1 of Management in everything you do: Manage others the way you would like to be managed."

—Brian Tracy

BEING A LEADER isn't for wimps. For some, it can be one of the toughest challenges they will ever face, but once you learn the techniques that truly work, your job can become much easier. Who wouldn't want to make their job easier while simultaneously becoming more successful? You won't find any "*Hero-to-Zero*" concepts included here, where you're a hero one month but a zero the next. You also won't read about any "*One-Hit-Wonder*" approaches, where you're a star one year but fall off everyone's radar soon after. These phenomena are far too common in sales, but together, we can banish them from the sales manager's playbook. My goal is to help you get into the Elite Club—and then *keep* you in that club for the rest of your career if you choose.

Starting at the Foundation

As with any good structure, it's best to start at the foundation to make sure your organization is built on rock-solid ground. The direction and success of your team both start with YOU. The foundation of leading top performance requires that you first fully understand and embrace the following key concept:

You work for your employees.
They don't work for you.

Those two sentences provide the ultimate foundation for building your Elite sales team. They also serve as the basis for becoming the type of manager who builds a team with techniques that promote long-term success, fierce team loyalty, and tremendous career satisfaction.

The peaks and valleys I experienced throughout my career revealed to me that teams don't work for their managers; they work for a bigger purpose. They work hard for themselves, their partner, kids, vacations, recognition, retirement, and for the monetary rewards that allow them to do and buy the things they want in life. They don't want to feel they are working hard to provide all of that for someone else. It's easy to fall into the trap of thinking that *THEY* work for *YOU*, but it really is just the opposite. Your job is to remove obstacles, resolve escalations, and be a friend, mentor, supporter, counselor, and more to your direct reports.

You need to be everything to everyone at all times, both UP and DOWN the organization chart.

It's an important job that comes with tremendous responsibility. I've actually witnessed some managers telling their teams that it is their job to hit their numbers so that the manager can make *his or her* quota. We know that is *not* the job of our teams. We want our people to exceed *their* quota, because if they achieve their quota, then we will achieve ours. That mindset is a much more effective way to drive Top Performance. My hope is that you're already using a team-centric philosophy, or that you choose to start using one now.

Our salespeople don't want us to tell them what they need to do at every single step of the way. I discovered that my Top Performers would always be clear when they needed my help. In fact, if given the choice, the majority of Top Performers would prefer to call their managers only when they needed something and would rather be left alone otherwise. In other words, most prefer a hands-off approach. The truly Elite performers want to sell more so they make more money—and they will find a way to do that faster when you are not standing over them.

You have tremendous power in your position as a leader. By providing the right training and encouragement, you can help people work to change their lives—financially, mentally, emotionally, and in ways you may never see. I know because years ago a manager helped me see my own potential. He had faith in me and hired me when he could have hired someone more qualified. That decision to trust in my potential helped me pay off a $40,000 debt not long after college and really changed my path in life.

Most of us have those one or two teachers from grade school, high school, or college who touched our lives in some profound, lasting way. As a sales leader, you have the same opportunity to influence and affect those who work around you. Your real influence is not based on the title on your business card. It's based on what you actually do with that title. You can start to assess what your leadership style is in the eyes of your team and how to begin utilizing your title in the most positive way by asking yourself:

- Am I using my leadership role to serve my ego or my wallet?
- Am I underutilizing my title, over-utilizing it, or using it appropriately?

- Am I using it so everyone *likes* me or to do my job to the best of my ability and be an example to those around me?

Is Your Thing Working?

Answering questions like the ones above is a good way to begin figuring what kind of leader you are, especially if you haven't given it much thought until now. Every leader has his or her *style*, those things that make you unique in a sea of other managers. While many of us have operated for years in the same style, as history proves, just because it's been done the same way for years doesn't mean it's the *best* way. So, it's time to answer the big question about yourself—the one you might have been avoiding: *Is my current management style really working for the range of personalities on my team?*

Others see us differently than we see ourselves, but don't expect to take a poll of your team and get honest answers. In the corporate world, most people feel they can't say what they really want to say about their leaders for fear of being judged, labeled, alienated, or retaliated against. That means it's up to us to figure out how we are perceived as leaders. Here are some other questions to get you thinking in the right direction:

- Am I authentic or do I sometimes come across as insincere?
- How important is it for me to get my way? Is it my way or the highway?
- Am I open to new ideas or do I shut them down?

- Do I interrupt people when they are talking or allow them to finish their thoughts?

The answers will begin to paint a clearer picture of how you are perceived and shed some light on what your brand is in the eyes of others. Your style will either enhance or interfere with your success—and you get to decide which it will be by how willing you are to change the elements that aren't working.

Something as simple as your choice of words or tone of voice can completely alter the way your team views you. I try to think carefully about my word choices and I expect others to choose their words wisely as well. If you hear, "Let me give you some criticism," or "Let me critique you," doesn't that makes you cringe? It's much nicer to say, "Let's talk about this." or "Can I share something?" It makes what you're about to say much more palatable.

Word choice matters:
Give feedback not criticism.
It's not what you say. It's how you say it.

Your tone of voice also plays a major role in "how you say it". I learned long ago to be consciously aware of the tone of my voice. When you keep your tone of voice at the top of your mind, it allows you to focus on not just the message itself, but also on how the message lands with the recipient.

Word choice can even affect your personal branding. I have removed the words *criticism, critique,* and many other words that carry a negative connotation from my vocabulary. I also avoid using always, never, YOU don't this and YOU don't that. There are so many other incredible words in the English language that will positively impact your team; and yes, it may seem like a small thing—but small word modifications and changes in your tone of voice can have a huge impact on your Elite status.

MANAGING WITH YOUR HEAD, HEART, OR FIST

I am living proof that you can have a heart in business and still drive top results. Having a heart doesn't mean you're weak. It shows that you're human. Having a heart doesn't mean others will lose respect for you. It means you can be even more respected and more effective. It IS possible. I have tried my hardest every day to prove it. At times, I got off course. I felt pressured by upper management to do or say certain things; but it was my duty to follow the direction of the company I worked for, so I did. Over time, I discovered that a softer hand—combined with targeted, positive coaching—spoke far more loudly and drove better results.

Individualized Management

Being an effective leader requires understanding the psychology of human beings—what makes them tick and what shuts them down. Elite leaders must also know how to lead their team members *individually*. People and their personalities are immensely diverse, which means that the best managers use multiple styles and techniques to get their messages across to the wide variety of styles and personalities on their teams. I strive to send the same message across the team, but I alter my delivery method based on knowing what works for each person. It boils down to this:

Same Message… Different Delivery.
Customize your message to fit each individual.

You need a style that works for you and gives your team the right to do the same. I realize this can be a challenging mission in the corporate environment because we're often told to treat everyone equally. When it comes to the idea that everyone must always be treated equally, I agree wholeheartedly that equality is important but when I used to try an identical approach for managing everyone, I found it to be highly ineffective. I've had leaders I reported to try to do the same to me. It was also highly ineffective.

Communicating in the same manner to each person on the team just didn't produce the results I wanted. It's no different than two children growing up in the same house—

their parents quickly learn that how they communicate and handle discipline with one child doesn't always work for the other one.

We have to learn what rows each person's boat and what gives them success on their *own* terms. Some will respond quickly to individualized management and become superstars seemingly overnight. Others may take more time, but once they get it, they too can become superstars. They may take different paths, but the end result is the same—and in the end, that's all we're really striving for. Your goal is to manage each person individually so they become a Top Performer in a way that is both constructive and sustainable. Encourage them to learn skills from other Top Performers and then create their own style based on those winning techniques.

Encourage and empower team members to do what works for THEM.

All Logic Means No Heart

Many old-school management techniques are based on all logic and no emotion. Maybe that approach worked a few decades ago, but in my experience, it's more acceptable and even productive to show human emotion in business today. In fact, for those who want to be part of the Elite, exhibiting our sentiments, excitement, and feelings with colleagues and clients is not an option. In order to foster the types of relationships that lead to top results, it simply must be done. It is also an imperative for Elite managers because your team will quickly discover that it's just not fun to work for people who manage with their head only and not their hearts. "All Logic, All the Time" doesn't inspire, and it doesn't motivate.

Leaders must be real.
Leaders must be authentic.

Being authentic means that you have to respect the authenticity of others as well. Seeing some people succeed while others are struggling is frustrating, and some managers respond to that frustration by trying to change those who are struggling into replicas of Top Performers. Unfortunately, I have found that to be a square-peg-in-a-round-hole approach. I advise my teams to go learn from the best and then transfer what they learn into their own style. If it's their *own* style, they'll actually use it.

What manager wouldn't love to clone Top Performers? After all, it's both natural and common to have favorites on your team and those favorites are often at the top of the leader boards. There are some people who fit better with your personality and your style than others will—and that's perfectly fine. The key is to be aware of who those favorites are and then remind yourself that although it seems logical and instinctive to favor your Top Performers, to do so is not acting in the best interests of the team as a whole.

One way to avoid displaying favoritism is to encourage all team members to share their questions and concerns. There will be times when it may be hard not to judge what you hear. However, if you remain open minded, you'll find what they're saying is often a clue to a real problem, a constructive solution, or a heartfelt emotion.

Forget Fear Management

It never fails—when underperformance occurs, some managers turn to leading by fear and micromanagement. As you have probably witnessed for yourself, that is a destructive strategy, because when the fist manages, everyone loses.

For starters, fear management reduces productivity because people are afraid to make mistakes, so they tend to take the safe route instead of taking necessary, innovative risks. Fear also prevents employees from learning from their mistakes, which lends them and your organization to repeat the same errors over and over again. Imagine how much more a team can accomplish when they aren't constantly looking over their shoulders waiting for the hammer to fall.

Managing by fear can also cause greater absenteeism and decreased employee satisfaction. After all, who wants to come to work when their manager points out very single mistake, embarrasses them in front of a group, and simply aren't happy?

If your company has a reputation of treating employees poorly, it's likely that you'll be challenged to hire and retain talented individuals. You may have to settle for second-stringers with little or no chance of becoming Top Performers. The few excellent prospects that do come onboard and join the team most likely won't stay for long. Once they realize the situation, they'll move on to greener pastures.

Common fear management techniques include:

- Threatening to quickly fire them if things don't change
- Frequent criticism
- Playing the "Blame Game"
- Focusing on what's wrong; never or rarely focusing on what's right
- "It's my way or the highway"

Do you use any of these? If you do, it's time to immediately remove them from your management playbook. Learn to leave managing through fear, demands, intimidation, and threats in the past. Instead, use encouragement, support, proper listening skills, an open mind, an open heart, and an overall positive approach to leadership.

When you remove fear management, it makes it easier to deal with the inevitable ups and downs of human emotion. We all have bad days, including you and everyone you work with. When you manage with your heart and remove the fear, you are able to recognize that if someone is having an especially rough day, things won't come crashing down if a key appointment or an important conference call has to be rescheduled. After all, I'd rather my people be on their A-game during the critical moments, not their F-game.

Good or bad day aside, there is simply no place for anger or fear tactics in Elite leadership. The great news is you don't need it anyway. If you have the right individuals on your team, you can trust that they will make up the time and work—and then some. Others may not care, but the Top Performers will always do what it takes to get back on track.

The Power of Having Their Back

Have a heart. Be authentic. Be positive. Be supportive. These may seem like self-explanatory principles that make perfect sense on paper, but are you actually utilizing and practicing them? More importantly: Does your team feel you're leading with your heart?

When you boil it down, we're all just humans with feelings and strong opinions, regardless of title or tenure. We all experience events in life such as relationship changes, moving, illness, childbirth, and more that can be huge distractions. Sometimes you know exactly what is going on in someone's life. Other times, you won't have a clue, and the only way you know something is wrong is because you'll see decreasing activity, decreasing sales, and inability to focus. When you approach your team as a friend and partner—rather than a boss—you'll see less and less of that anger, those mood swings, and that feeling of distance. My own career proved that you could still be a friend *and* drive results.

Be their ally.
Have their back.

Understand that "Life Happens" to everyone, so practice being flexible. Leading with your heart isn't a weak approach—*it's an effective approach.* It shows people that you care and that you want them to be successful. It creates a safe place in which your team is comfortable enough to share things and get other burning issues off their chest from time to time.

So what does it mean to have your team's back? Some examples include:

- Give team members the benefit of the doubt if a client throws them under the bus and help find a solution that makes the client happy. All too often I see managers get angry and reprimand a rep without hearing their version of what happened. Always be sure to get both sides of the story—one from the client and one from your direct report. When I was managing Elite Sales Teams, if a client called, before I jumped to a conclusion or sided with the client, I would always contact the rep to get their version before deciding what to do.

- Escalate issues you may not always agree with to let your team know you're doing all you can to support them. This doesn't mean our teams always get their way, but showing you're making the effort will mean a lot to them.
- Stick up and fight for your team when it comes to anything from commission payout errors, to customer issues, to territory poaching, to issues with upper management.

Sales is a wild world, and things don't always go as we planned. We could get an exciting agreement from a sizable client one day, only to be notified the next day that the deal has fallen apart. When your team knows you have their backs during the good and the bad—it is *priceless*. Knowing that I have their backs at all times also happens to be the one thing that my teams have told me they valued the most year after year.

Having someone's back can be tricky. It's definitely not something that happens overnight. To me, it's a right that is earned. When you get to know your team better, as an Elite leader you won't be content to stand on the sidelines and say, "Sorry, this is your fight, not mine." Instead, you'll want to jump right in and do everything you can to help your team.

Over time and with consistency, your team will instinctively believe that you will side with them when the going gets tough. That will foster tremendous confidence, trust, and respect. My teams have thanked me again and again for giving them this kind of unwavering support. When done right, this support becomes a two-way street, as they show you they have your back by hitting their numbers, submitting requests on time, responding to things you need, showing respect, displaying cooperation, and being a loyal friend.

I will always ensure that my teams know I have their back, partly because I have spent much of my life without anyone having mine. My career has been filled with many achievements, but unfortunately it wouldn't take more than one hand to count the number of times I was recognized for them. When times were tough, fire drills were frequent, and problems loomed, all I ever wanted to hear was "*Thank You.*" It would have been encouraging for my leader to acknowledge that he/she saw how much I'd overcome to rise to the top. I wanted to hear something heartfelt and sincere, but I rarely did.

It's amazing how many leaders don't say "Thank you," or say it way too infrequently. I've been guilty of it myself on occasion. Work gets so busy that we can forget to slow down to show some appreciation and give verbal praise. But we *do* have time. It only takes a few seconds in most cases. So say it verbally, in writing, and where and when appropriate, say it publically. Take someone to lunch and tell others during team calls or meetings—if they have indicated that they like public praise. However you deliver the message, decide to start letting your team know how much you appreciate their hard work and effort. It will make all the difference in strengthening the relationships within your team.

Lead with your heart and have their backs. I'm here to tell you it can work—and it can drive results. The days of managing by fear, demand, intimidation, and threat are long gone. A heart-led approach based on a *genuine* desire to see others succeed is absolutely one of the best ways to keep your team motivated. They crave the chance to work with someone real, authentic, and trustworthy—and that's an important point, because one of the most common questions I get asked is, "How do I keep my people motivated?" My heartfelt answer is you shouldn't have to. Motivation is short lived for the majority. And leading from the heart isn't about giving people empty praise or an "I Believe in You!" speech. For the Elite, motivation is an innate trait that's on autopilot. Yet your positive, encouraging appreciation lends greatly to it.

People either have motivation or they don't.

Something may motivate you for a minute, an hour, or a year after you read it, receive it, or experience it. But if your team members need *you* to be their primary source of motivation, you've likely hired the wrong fit for the job. You won't need to continually motivate if you hire right, lead with your heart, and support your team through the peaks and valleys of their careers.

MUTING THE MICROMANAGEMENT BUTTON

I see it happen frequently. Times get tough, sales results drop, panic sets in, and sales leaders instantly turn into obsessive micromanagers. It may seem like a logical response. But this antiquated approach of control and manipulation is outdated. It's dangerous and can actually make the situation worse.

Micromanagement could have unintended consequences. Instead of getting people in line, it may cause them to leave.

I've yet to come across a single person who enjoys being micromanaged. Yet some leaders still default to it because that's the way they were taught, or perhaps they feel they have to because their leaders do it to them. It's easy to fall back on micromanagement because it gives us a feeling of control. However, the control is an illusion and the damage it does can often be irreparable. The good news is there is a plethora of progressive, innovative methods that exist to take its place. Here are a few actions that worked well for me to help eradicate micromanagement from the leadership playbook:

- **Focus on boosting activity.** Have strategic conversations about activity with a focus on boosting numbers by discussing what's working, what they're doing right, and areas of improvement. When you identify an area of concern, be sure to encourage rather than condemn.

- **Go back to basics.** Take a look at their sales process. Review the number of calls they are making to get appointments, the number of appointments they are booking, and the number of deals they close. Then ask them to deliver their presentation to you. Are they asking for the sale? Are they too timid or too aggressive? Are they *product dumping*—listing features and benefits of the product or service in excruciating detail—instead of engaging in consultative selling?
- **Weed out the culprits.** Identify if something is distracting them, either at work or at home. Consider the possibility that they do not have sufficient activity to support the numbers and results expected. It may also be that they are working smart but not hard, or working hard but not smart.
- **Discover workspace problems**. Observe the state of their physical working environment to determine whether they are working in a positive and healthy environment that promotes productivity. This can be underestimated.
- **Uncover peer influencers.** Investigate to determine whether one of their peers is unknowingly

negatively impacting them or contributing to some type of distraction.

- **Get to the real issue.** Sometimes you just need to find the answer to one question: Do they really want to be there?

People want to know and feel they've earned the right to *not* be micromanaged. Top Performers have earned that right and they usually don't need a lot of cheerleading to stay at the top. If you do feel that you have to micromanage, you likely have the wrong hire. No style of management can help someone who is not a fit for the job. Most of the time that individual knows it and it becomes your job to help him or her make the choice to be IN or OUT. Just like it is with any relationship, why stay if it isn't working? The employee deserves a position he or she really wants and you deserve a better hire. It's time for us to press MUTE on the micromanaging button, because that's exactly what people do to us when we start micromanaging them.

YOUR NEW SET OF ELITE EXPECTATIONS

Expectations or Free Range?

Setting high expectations is a must to get big results. When it comes to achieving Elite status, I quickly recognized that my teams had to know exactly what I expected from them and from myself at all times. I created several standards for performance that everyone on the team had to live up to. The following three expectations were a driving force in every team I have led:

1. **100% Productivity.** I set the expectation on my teams that <u>every</u> member needs to be at or above his or her quota—***period***—and I recommend you do the same. In order to make this a reality, I always focused on strategically figuring out unique ways for each individual to hit his or her goal. Why? Because I know that if each person on my team achieves or exceeds their quota, I will make mine. There is a commonly accepted business standard in the corporate world called the "Pareto Principle." This principle states that 80% of all productivity comes from the efforts of just 20% of the people involved. I know that is the way we are *supposed* to think about our teams—that a handful of them are the only ones who actually contribute to the bottom line—but why think the same as everyone else? A more effective, comprehensive message I have learned to convey is this: 100% of the team must contribute to 100% of the team productivity. It doesn't always happen yet typically it helps you as a leader over-achieve your goals.

2. **100% Participation.** I also expect everyone on my team to fully participate in meetings and group calls. It's unfair for one or two people to always carry

the weight for the others. I even assume my team members will *gladly* share success principles, tips, and strategies with others on the team to foster team building and growth. It's a team effort. Get everyone to pitch in and it will add value to meetings, conversations, and to the team as a whole. No one can or should try to climb to the top alone, whether in sports or sales. Create an environment where the team wants to help train, sell, and share best practices, and then ensure that you recognize and acknowledge them for doing so.

3. **Zero Tolerance on Key Issues.** I have a zero-tolerance policy for lack of performance, bad attitudes, negativity, and unethical behavior. No one could ever accuse my teams or me of achieving our numbers through doing anything unethical. Elite performers have *integrity*. Reinforce that you and your people must do the right thing, even when no one's watching. Don't try to manipulate the system or give guidance that crosses ethical boundaries. Crossing the lines of integrity will always come back to haunt you. I have always found it's best to sell with integrity and accept nothing less from your team.

Everyone needs boundaries and expectations, from infants to adults. Your team is no exception. Drawing boundaries will help you figure out your stance on issues stemming from tardiness to lack of performance or responsiveness to your policy on the number of hours you expect your team to work each day. Boundaries also provide benchmarks for proper treatment and expected response times on issues like after-hours emails and other communications.

Top Performance requires different thinking and different strategies.

Setting boundaries that have universal application makes your job so much simpler. Never again will you need to remember whose standard to judge a particular situation by because everyone will know that they are expected to behave according to the same standards that have been set for the entire team.

Is Workaholism Working?

I am no stranger to overtime, but after spending countless hours working nights and weekends, I realized something. I discovered that I could still have success without working fourteen-hour days. The work will *always* be there. I eventually had to take personal responsibility and stop the insanity. I began to see it as my "responsibility" to work a reasonable number of hours a week because I recognized that whatever I did, my team thought they had to do it that way, too.

The urge to be a workaholic can be powerful. I have damaged relationships, friendships, and my health due to working too many hours. Perhaps you experienced this as well at some point in your career. I have also lost myself on occasion. There were times when I looked back and realized that ninety percent or more of my days were spent working, and the rest of the time was spent sleeping. What kind of life is that?

I first learned a lesson about enjoying more of life's moments at the age of seventeen. My dad got up one morning, went to work, and never came home. He died of a massive heart attack before I even had a chance to say goodbye. He was a hardworking, industrious man, and I will forever thank him for instilling a strong work ethic in me. I am also grateful to him for reminding me that life isn't all about work, but that is still something I struggle with and need to be extraordinarily conscious of managing.

I know I won't look back on my life and my career during my golden years and be proud of how many hours I worked each week. I want to remember exploring the world through travel, the precious moments with loved ones, as well as the accomplishments. You can still be highly effective without working 24/7, 20/6, or 60/5. I urge you to spend more time with your family and friends. You never know how much time you have with any of them.

How many hours are you working? What will be your new shutdown time? And how will you benefit?

No job is worth sacrificing your health or your relationships. If you don't have your health or relationships, you don't have anything. I've grieved the loss of my father, mother, friends, and other relatives, and toward the end of their lives, all of them have said the one thing they would have changed was how much they worked compared to how much they stopped to smell the roses. You can still have success without marrying your job and without sacrificing your *actual* marriage, family, friends, or health.

I believe that vacations are as much a part of work as your work is. They revive you, recharge you, and give you reasons to work harder. Be the kind of leader who encourages vacations and time off from the grind.

I have not always been lucky enough to have the kind of leader who encouraged taking personal time. In fact, under one particular leader, I was forced to plan all my trips abroad because he expected me to work during my vacations if I went somewhere on this continent.

When I planned a vacation to Italy, he actually asked how he could get in touch with me. I was stunned. Another leader got upset when I didn't respond by 8a.m. on Monday morning to an email she sent at 6p.m. the previous Friday night. Don't be like those leaders. They may have good intentions, but they just come across as overbearing. Here are two ways to avoid being that kind of leader:

1. **Don't Work on Vacation.** Develop a policy that when you go on vacation or take a day off, you DON'T work. Vacation means vacation. I literally have to put my cell phone, iPad®, and laptop in a drawer so I cannot see or touch them.
2. **Give Your Email a Break (or a Vacation).** Stop sending and replying to emails when you're supposed to be taking time off. This sends the messages that your team must respond to emails while on vacation.

We need to learn from the Europeans. Their work isn't their life—nor should your work be your life. The absence of a healthy work/life balance will eventually take its toll on you. Unfortunately, the corporate world is guilty of making people feel they need to be working around the clock.

But you can make the choice to start making a positive change now—for yourself and others well being. Even the best racehorses need to rest.

You can't run at your maximum if you're always pushing your limits. Neither can your team.

ELITE SALES LEADER ESSENTIALS

It may seem like there is no end to the list of attributes you must possess in order to become a member of the Elite group—the ones who consistently remain at the top of the ranking reports.

While there are many ingredients in the recipe for leadership success, there are three qualities no Elite sales leader can be without:

You must be Dependable.
You must be on Top of your Game.
You must Drive Top Results.

The best leaders are those who lead by example by posting top numbers themselves. When you remain a Top Performer even after you assume a leadership position, you can more easily identify ways to make everyone's work more streamlined and productive because you are still out in the trenches along with the rest of the team. Be the kind of leader who stays at the top of their game and who leads by example by being in the field. When you witness the action from the frontlines of your business, it provides you with valuable perspective and insight that you could never have from behind a desk.

In addition to leading by example, you must be the dependable rock that your team relies on for coaching and training. Work to provide new tools, useful resources, and ongoing training to your team—and not just when they are new hires. Such resources could be in the form of internal support, detailed account information, or lists of companies for them to target. It could also mean making yourself more available. Be there to help and to serve. It will often come back to you tenfold.

Have Those Tough Conversations

Part of your job—which you won't actually see in any job description—is that you will have to initiate some tough conversations during your career. Such conversations may come in the form of having a heart-to-heart with a struggling rep, disciplining an employee who is negatively impacting your working relationship or the team, getting someone back on track after a quarter of mediocre performance, and of course, the toughest one of all, letting someone go.

No one likes tough conversations. They can be uncomfortable and create tension—but they are necessary and should be handled as soon as possible. Putting them off will only make the situation worse. While not everyone is open to feedback, there are constructive ways to have tough conversations and there are destructive ways that will do more harm than good. A leader of mine once scheduled a call with me from 4:30p.m.-5:00p.m. on a Friday and criticized me for the duration of the call. There are several reasons why that Friday afternoon call from my leader is an example of what not to do:

- You know the old adage, "Never go to bed angry." In the corporate world, it's more like, "Never leave work angry." My manager insulted me for thirty minutes at 4:30p.m. on a Friday and then expected me to happily hang up the phone to go have a pleasant weekend without experiencing the emotions that naturally stem from being unfairly criticized. That should not have happened. Tough one-on-ones should not be scheduled as the last item on the day's agenda or the first thing in the morning.
- It's best not to deliver negative feedback over the phone if you have the option to deliver it face-to-face. Sometimes the phone may be the only way to communicate with a team member (as in the case of virtual teams), but if at all possible, have tough conversations in person.
- My manager never stopped for air. He went on for thirty minutes without ever allowing me to contribute a response, comment, or question. Don't treat feedback sessions like a one-way monologue. Treat them as two-way conversations and you'll be more likely to actually be heard. Allow the recipient time and respect to respond.

There will be other times when it seems like every conversation you have with a team member is a tough conversation. Some people are more difficult to manage than others, but you cannot assume that if a person is a "difficult" person, it automatically means he or she is not a fit on your team. I've had numerous Top Performing salespeople on my teams who required the use of kid gloves during conversations and were in general more difficult than others. But they were still strong, contributing members of the team. The key is to treat everyone with respect and honest intention. After awhile, even tough conversations with the difficult people will become a little easier.

Just remember, if tough conversations aren't presented properly, they can go wrong quickly. Here are a few other tips for handling your next tough conversation:

1. Prior to the tough conversation, prepare notes and strategically decide *how* you will deliver difficult feedback or news. Will it be in-person or by phone? Also decide *when* and *where* you'll deliver the information. A neutral location is often a good place to deliver unpleasant news and be sure to keep it factual.
2. Ask the other person to tell you how he or she feels so it becomes a two-way conversation.
3. Remain calm. Remove the emotions and stick with the facts. Don't let the conversation get heated or emotional. If it does, bring it back to the facts and

don't allow passions to escalate. My teams have heard me say numerous times, "Let's take out the emotions and talk about the facts." If you sense that the individual has become too irrational during the exchange, professionally state that you'd like to finish the conversation at another time.

4. Try to avoid scheduling tough conversations on a Monday morning or a Friday afternoon. Be aware that that if you have an encounter early in the day, an employee may not work the rest of that day or the next depending on the severity of the news you deliver.
5. Don't wing it. You need to know what you are going to say and you also need to have responses planned for some of the questions you expect the person to have. Just like when we are face-to-face with a prospect, our presentations and conversations run more smoothly when we aren't struggling to find the right words, so make notes and bullet points to use. Have no more than one to three points maximum to cover in one conversation and stick to the facts.
6. Demonstrating that you still care about the person and his or her future with the company is key. Let people know you have their best interests and the best interests of the team in mind, not your own. Showing that you care also involves choosing what's important enough to address and what to just let go.

Some things just aren't worth it. You must clearly decide what to let go.

7. Find that fine line between being so positive that you come across as insincere and being able to be real and share what's on your mind. I have worked for cold, unfeeling leaders who knew nothing about me, nor I about them. The only way to really care about someone is to know something about him or her. Be a real person, and learn that it's okay to let people know a few non-invasive things about you.

Elite Leaders Never Stop Seeking

The best leaders are the ones who don't view their daily tasks as duties; they see them as privileges. Even though there will be days when you don't feel like leading, that is simply not an option. Always look around for ways to make your team's days run a little more smoothly. Can you help resolve problems for your team such as customer service escalations, client complaints, personnel issues, and more? Or will you choose to ignore them in the hopes that they'll disappear? One surefire way to demotivate your team is to be unresponsive or not respond in a timely manner to their calls and emails. Be responsive and proactive. It will convey the fact that you care about them and their success, and it will go a long way toward moving you from the middle to the top.

Your attitude is a subject for much discussion, but for the sake of brevity, remember this: *Even when you are feeling negative, be positive.* This is important because if you are tired, they'll hear and feel your exhaustion. If you're worried, they'll sense it and may become worried themselves. I don't have a "Pollyanna" view of life or the job and I don't see everything through rose-colored glasses. I simply try to maintain a positive, upbeat demeanor with my teams at all times. When you're down, they are. If you get emotional, they may become emotional as well. On the other hand, if you stay strong, they will stay strong. If you're positive, they will try to look on the bright side as well. With all they have to handle when it comes to their prospects and customers, they'll appreciate coming to a leader who remains upbeat.

One of the best ways to improve others is to continually improve you. Perhaps the most valuable lessons I learned in life I learned from doing exactly what you are doing right now. Over the years, I've spent thousands of dollars on personal and professional development. I've read countless books, attended countless seminars and conferences for business and personal growth, and worked with mentors, coaches, and leaders. I know unequivocally this has had a direct impact on my professional growth and success. It has also led directly to my ability to make more of that one thing we all want most.

There is never a time in my career when I have stopped pursuing personal growth and development. There are endless resources available to us today through the Internet. If you are more traditional, just open a book and read about what worked for someone else. I never want to try to reinvent any wheel that someone else out there has already invented. In other words, let others figure out all the ways *not* to do something and then allow them to show you the ways to do it right the first time.

If you don't think you have time for doing any outside reading, going to seminars, or hiring your own coach, I encourage you to reconsider. We can always become better versions of ourselves; and for my part, I plan to keep improving for as long as I'm still here.

IT'S YOUR TURN

Managing isn't for the faint of heart. We're a special tribe. Now I want to give you some food for thought that will help you determine your current management style and how you can make it even better. As you answer these questions, be honest (don't worry, no one is looking over your shoulder):

Identify your primary management style based on what you learned in the chapter. If they were asked anonymously, would your team say your current style is working for your team? Why or why not?

____

____

____

How would you describe your current work style? If your team were asked anonymously, would they agree or would it differ?

____

____

____

Are you providing your team with right training and knowledge to succeed? What more can you do to help your team achieve their goals?

____

____

____

Do you ever default to micromanagement? Moving forward, what will you do to avoid micromanaging? What can you replace micromanaging with?

____

____

____

How do you give feedback or initiate tough conversations? Is your feedback style direct or passive? Is it comfortable for you, or do you avoid it at all costs? What could you do to improve it?

____

____

____

Are you emailing and calling after hours and/or on weekends? Will you commit to change this and when?

____

____

____

Are you setting clear, comprehensive performance expectations individually and with your team?

____

____

____

What things do you do that show your team you have their back? What things would you like to do?

____

____

____

One of the greatest ways to improve others is to continually improve your own self. Are you investing in personal growth and development, such as reading, seminars, and coaching? If not, what kinds of self-improvement can you commit to today?

____

____

____

SECRET 2

IT'S ALL ABOUT THE TEAM

THE RIGHT PLAYERS ARE RANKING RISERS

"A small team of A-plus players can run circles around a giant team of B and C players."

—Steve Jobs

IF YOU'VE BEEN in sales or management for any length of time, you know that Top Performers seem to have that *thing*, that innate drive, that makes them better than the rest—and much of the time, it has little to do with you or anything you have done or said to them. You've probably also noticed a funny thing happen once Top Performers earn the recognition and payoff that comes with being at the top of the ranking report:

Once an Elite performer gets a taste of being at the top, they won't want to drop.

It would be ideal if you had an entire team of Top Performers who felt that way. It would also be great if your team had perfect energy and synergy, and loved, respected, and supported their teammates at all times. We know we don't live in a perfect world, but there are elements of an ideal scenario you can reach for and start to expect from your team.

Before you can reach for the stars, however, you need to evaluate your team's strengths and weaknesses. In fact, it's critical to do this on an ongoing basis—especially after any turnover occurs. You may think you know where your vulnerabilities lie, but without consciously doing an assessment, you may be trying to fix issues where none exist while overlooking the real issues altogether.

Another reason this is important is because you must strive to build your own team culture and team brand—one that exists independent of the company culture. Your team culture needs to align with the overall company culture, but with *your* spin that makes the team unique to its members and your leadership style. Performing an assessment sets the tone for how you plan to run your team.

When I begin working with a sales team, I ask two questions that help me determine who I am working with, what they bring to the table, and where my assets and liabilities exist so that I can begin to form our team identity and strategies. You can easily do the same, and those questions are the topics of the next two sections.

Are They Actually Working?

The first question to ask about every member of the team is, "Is this person really working?" It seems simple enough to read those words on paper, yet this step is often missed. When I ask this question and discover the answer is "not working," then the next step is to figure out why. If they *are* working, identify if they are working as effectively as possible. They could be working overtime only to get nowhere. Here's a helpful clue to speed the entire process along:

"In the office" means they're not working.

Some may not agree with me on that. I've worked for my share of leaders who felt adamantly that you were only working if you were *in* the office. I will acknowledge that there are certain positions in the world of sales that require time on the phone, in front of a laptop, or in meetings. In my opinion, if you are in outside sales, the vast majority of your teams workday should be spent in the field, not in an office.

Being in the office can be a stifling career move. I've worked virtually and have managed many virtual teams. I'll bet big money that people who *aren't* stuck in the office work far more hours than they would if they were *in* the office. In fact, it's harder to shut it down when you know you have 24-hour access to your work.

One technique to determine whether your team is really working is to take note of when they send and reply to emails. Is it during prime prospecting hours? You can also review their activity reports on a regular basis and establish whether they are consistent each week or month. Over time, you may see patterns and trends that display the trademark inconsistencies and inefficiencies of someone who is not really working.

Do I Have the Right People?

The second question to answer is, "Do I have the *right* team members?" Salespeople are truly unique. We see the world differently than those who have the nine-to-five desk jobs of the world. That unique aspect can make identifying Top Performers a little tricky, but there are some overt signs of Top Performance that I have identified over the years. My experience is this:

Successful sales reps can either be the easiest to lead or the most difficult to lead.

My best performers were either autonomous powerhouses or extremely high maintenance. I'll never really know why this has been the case, but regardless, it's been a consistent trend at every company I've worked for—odd but true.

By far, the most reliable way to figure out whether you've hired the right people is to start by reviewing their performance. Look at their results over the last month, quarter, and year. It's not about how much you like them or how much you enjoy their charming personality. Remove how you feel about them personally and examine performance alone, using the following grading system:

- **A= Absolutely.** I know this person can over-achieve and has consistently exceeded goals.
- **B= Believe.** I believe this person can be an over-achiever, but he or she may need some additional help, focus, and coaching to get there. Their performance is consistent and they regularly exceed goals.
- **C= Could.** I believe this person could have what it takes to be at the top, but I'm not completely sure yet. I need to observe activity for a little longer. Their performance is inconsistent.
- **D= Don't Believe So.** I don't believe this person will be able to make it in the long run even if provided additional help and training. I don't believe this person is the right fit for the job. They rarely exceed goals and often struggle in some areas.

- **F= Forget About It.** I've tried everything to help this person rise to the top, but coaching, training, support, and mentoring has not worked. They consistently under perform. I'm confident this person is the wrong fit for the job.

Use this system to grade team members on any aspect of their skill set, desire, and internal drive. The point of this grading method is to provide you with a systematic way to categorize your team. After reviewing the black-and-white, statistical facts and figures, you can identify whether they are Low Performers, Average Performers, or Top Performers.

How would you grade each direct report? To get started using this grading system, consider the following statements in regard to each member of your team, and after each, grade using the A-F scale on how well the statement applies to each team member and his or her performance:

They have the skill set needed to be a Top Performer:

A B C D F

They have the desire and the drive to succeed:

A B C D F

Their actions back up their stated desire to succeed:

A B C D F

They are open-minded and will listen to coaching and feedback, and then take what others say and apply it:

A B C D F

For Top Performers with all A's, there is no action necessary. Just help them continue to do what they are already doing. If they are not Top Performers, you have a decision to make:

You must decide whether to move them up, over, or out.

Sometimes the decision is clear. If they are Low Performers, you more than likely need to move them ***out*** or to another position. You will need to move fast if you want to move someone out. Depending on your specific HR policies and company size, it may take months to manage an underperforming employee out of the company. It may also take months to do a proper assessment, which is why a systematic, non-biased grading system is required to maintain your focus on their performance.

Sometimes the decision is not so clear. If you still cannot decide what kind of fit you have after looking at the hard facts, you must then take the intangibles into consideration, such as attitude, likeability with clients, willingness to grow and improve, the relationship between you and the individual, and the relationship between the person and the team. These are not all the intangible criteria to consider, but they will get you thinking about the soft skills that matter most.

First and foremost, look at productivity and sales skills. That is the best and least biased way to determine whether you have a clear winner, a diamond in the rough, or someone who may need to find another position. Those two questions "Are they actually working?" and "Do I have the right people?" have done more good for my teams than any complex, expensive team assessments ever could. Always remember to go back to the basics: For your salespeople, that means activity. For leaders, that means finding the honest answers to those two key questions.

BUSY VERSUS PRODUCTIVE

We've focused on the importance of examining tangible indicators of success, and now an important distinction must be made. Being *busy* is not the same thing as being *productive.* The term "busy work" has a negative connotation for good reason. Being busy won't guarantee that you will post better numbers and get better results, but being productive almost certainly will. As you examine the following categories, ask yourself whether your team members are being busy or being productive.

Assess Their Activity

When you lead salespeople, you must track activity and do so consistently. The world of professional selling lives and dies by activity. You can best identify whether they have the *right* activity that will close enough business to meet their quotas by looking at the facts. Here are some of the first facts I ascertain about each salesperson's activity:

- **What is their daily schedule?** Get the breakdown of how they are spending their time—in their territory, in the office, on the phone, and with clients. Identify what activities consume the majority of their time.
- **Are they getting in front of enough clients?** You can easily determine this by monitoring the number of weekly and monthly appointments they conduct.
- **Are they good in front of clients?** Evaluate how effective they are during their face-to-face meetings with clients. This may require shadowing some calls. After which, you can provide some positive, specific, and helpful feedback that will help them improve.
- **Are they closing enough deals?** Monitor the number and size of deals they close versus the number of appointments they attend. Put the results in a spreadsheet and calculate the actual percentages to review with them.
- **Can everyone see peer performance?** Post numbers in the office or send them via email for all to see. Posting numbers in public becomes an unspoken motivator. No one wants to see his or her name on the bottom of any ranking. By making the information public and transparent, you add a silent and powerful accountability factor to results.

By analyzing data, it is easier to determine who is and isn't working effectively—and who wants you to believe they are working—based on facts. If your company is already using some form of sales automation or CRM (customer relationship management) software, those types of tools make this process much simpler. If you aren't, start requesting that activity reports be sent to you weekly for analysis.

The proof lies in the number of deals they close.

When reviewing activity reports, it's important to note and stay on top of activity-to-close ratios. Most reps won't, so it's up to you to take on this responsibility. If a rep has a low activity rate and high close rate, encourage them to increase their activity with an eye to closing even more sales. If a rep has a high activity rate and low close rate, work with them to clearly identify why they aren't closing more deals.

I once had a rep that posted a high number of appointments but had a very low closing rate. When I brought this to his attention, he realized he was so focused on getting new appointments that he wasn't following up with the prospects he had already met with. As a result, he wasn't closing deals. I suggested he reconnect with every prospect he had recently met with. When he did, he closed five deals that month.

Becoming a manager who analyzes data is not the same as being the kind of manager who thrives on metrics alone. It's important to determine who has low activity-to-close ratios and who has high activity-to-close ratios, but I've seen many Top Performing individuals post relatively low activity, and yet close a lot of deals.

This goes back to the principle of Individualized Management: No one can be managed in the exact same manner as another. Use metrics as a starting point for analysis, but don't let the numbers do *all* the talking. Your people are far more than their numbers.

Pursue Their Pipeline

A healthy, robust pipeline is another vital aspect of activity. If a salesperson is closing ten deals this week, but has nothing on the horizon for the rest of the quarter, that kind of inconsistency is a problem. Pull ninety-day pipeline reports and review them individually. Do they have a robust or weak pipeline? Weed through the forecast to identify the legitimate opportunities from the artificial ones. Here are some questions that will help you examine their pipelines with greater efficiency:

- Who is the ultimate decision maker? Have they met with this person? If so, how many times?
- Who are additional influencers in their company? Have they met with them? If so, how many times? Have they asked these people to help them meet with the ultimate decision maker?

- Who writes the check?
- Do they have the budget for this?
- Why would they want to buy from us?
- What could prevent them from buying?
- What's the probability they'll buy from us in the next thirty/sixty/ninety days?
- ***And my favorite...*** "Would you bet $100 that this deal will close this month?"

If you ask the right questions, you can quickly and effectively assess whether someone is working wisely. If someone has difficulty answering questions like the ones above, then it's time to start questioning what that person is really doing with his or her time. It is also a golden opportunity to course-correct to get them back on the success track.

Countless salespeople have told me (and probably you) that customer service issues consume the majority of their selling time. Help your team avoid this time trap by reminding them their job is to sell, not to be customer service reps. Customer service is a huge part of closing and maintaining deals, but in order to achieve Top Performance, your team must be highly effective at managing these issues and at delegating appropriately. They need more time to sell and less time dealing with customer service issues or putting out fires.

Evaluate Their Environment

Do your salespeople work in a home office, virtual office, corporate office space, or some combination? The best office is the one that promotes productivity and positivity. While there may be no one-size-fits-all ideal office, there are certainly some aspects that make for a bad working environment. For starters, here's an easy formula for identifying an unhealthy environment:

Dog Barking + Baby Crying = Bad Environment

That seems like a no-brainer to most of us, right? Well, by having a candid conversation with one of my managers, I found out he was working virtually out of his bedroom while his wife and kids played throughout the house. While he prospected on the phone, top executives could hear his kids screaming and his dog barking in the other room.

A home office is productive only if such distractions are not present, but home offices aren't the only places where distractions can exist. Office spaces can be filled with disgruntled, overworked employees who don't want to be there. Offices are also filled with idle chatter and loud talkers, and in an open office environment (i.e. a sea of cubicles or a large room with desks) this can be even more distracting than a barking dog.

In fact, many salespeople feel that the open offices typically occupied by sales reps add their own set of challenges in the form of personality clashes that are hard to escape due to the lack of personal space. Not to mention they provide little to no privacy for prospecting and making important client calls. Offices can also become gossip mills, which can damage both productivity and relationships.

Such distractions and issues with office spaces may lead some managers to conclude that a virtual office is the answer, but managing a virtual team brings with it some unique challenges. I spent the majority of my career working virtually and managing virtual workers, so I'm well aware of the pros and cons and what it takes to succeed in a virtual environment.

Managing a working environment when your team doesn't have an actual office requires a different approach. Salespeople rarely, if ever, see one another, and some can feel a real sense of isolation and a lack of support, while others thrive in this environment.

In order to manage people who are 100% virtual, you must make sure that you are available even though you may not actually see each other on a regular basis. Keep your presence known, while allowing your team the freedom to run their business with an entrepreneurial mindset. If possible, meet with each rep in person from time to time. To make the best use of everyone's time, you can turn in-person time into a teaching opportunity by going out in the field for client appointments. You may also consider scheduling monthly team lunches if distance allows, and reserve time in the agenda for team building so it's not all work and no play.

Whether your team is based in an office or virtually, organize regular meetings with individuals and the entire team both by phone and face-to-face whenever possible. Team meetings don't have to be a waste of everyone's time if you establish a clear agenda for each meeting and set the expectation that each meeting requires 100% participation. During meetings, allocate time to encourage informal conversations and invite your team to share their best practices, new ideas, challenges, and successes to help build relationships and trust between members.

It will be challenging for your team to be Top Performers if they aren't working in the right environment to succeed. The right environment is supportive and positive, whether it's virtual or office based. Help them recognize and remove distractions in order to get them into a work environment that promotes success and remarkable achievement.

NAILING YOUR PITCH

Activity is always the primary indicator I rely on to determine why a salesperson is or is not a Top Performer—but it doesn't stop there. You can easily have a team member who works hard, but who doesn't seem to be able to climb the ranking reports. It's the kind of person who spins his or her wheels and may get the engine running for a few minutes, but when the dust settles, is right where he or she started. In my experience, this comes down to two things: First, this is a classic example of a person working hard, not smart. Second, the individual is not properly prepared to do the job correctly.

Your sales reps spend valuable time and energy to secure appointments, so it's critical that they make every one count. How good are they once they get in front of clients? Do they make it or break it? It's your responsibility as a leader to find out and help them improve.

It All Hinges on Preparation

No matter how good your product or service is or how much you just *know* people need it, your ability to pitch is even more important than the actual merits of the product or service. The pitch is only as effective as the material it contains and the way it is delivered. Your team must know why clients would want to buy from them and why they would stay with your company in the long term. This is an integral part of every salesperson's success because:

Nailing your pitch equals money in your pocket and your name at the top of the ranking report.

Nailing the pitch is the best way to ensure that clients buy and then keeping buying. I've seen salespeople make a sale, but soon hear that the client quickly switched to a competitor. If your sales team does the proper job of finding real needs and then sells the value and benefits of your product, service, and company, you won't experience that kind of frequent churn. You will experience better retention, happier clients, and more high quality referrals.

If you undergo excessive client turnover, it's likely your product or service isn't being sold or positioned powerfully enough. To undercover the reason, you'll need to spend quality time identifying where the gap exists and coach your employee to a higher and more effective skill set.

Depending on your specific product, service, and industry this may vary but it can be used as a general guideline. The opening should tell the client who you are and why you're there in the first place. The beginning of the pitch is also when you start to establish rapport and build trust by showing that you are there to find out how you can help them and prove that you are an expert on the matter. The opening is not a time to product dump, which is far too common for salespeople to do. Trust takes time to grow, but it has to take root somewhere; the opening moments provide you with that opportunity.

The meat of the pitch is filled with all the features and benefits your clients need and want. *Don't mistake this for product dumping.* Product dumping is a natural tendency for most salespeople—for new recruits and seasoned reps. People get excited about their product or service and can't wait to list ALL the reasons to buy. They end up neglecting to ask prospects *why* they want their product or service or find out what their offering could do to solve a problem that exists for their prospects.

**Don't product dump.
Sell value and benefits
important to the client.**

I'll never forget an appointment I attended with a new rep where he product dumped on the prospect for the duration of the meeting. When he was done, the client looked at him, shook his head, and said, "Do you even know what my company does?" This was embarrassing. It's important to have product knowledge, but just because you know the ins and outs of your product or service doesn't mean every last detail should be shared with your prospects. In other words:

**Product knowledge does not
necessarily equal success.**

Product dumping is one of the best ways to sabotage your chances of making the sale. A few years ago, I decided to buy a new car. At the dealership, the salesman kept trying to sell me on the convenience of being able to fold the back seats down so that I could fit my skis in the car. Nice feature. Unfortunately, *I don't ski.* He was dumping instead of consulting. Had he simply asked me the right qualifying questions, he would have had me signing the paperwork in no time.

If he had been smart, he would have asked what kind of car I was looking for and what was important to me. He would have found out I am a golfer and talked about solving the problem of my golf clubs not fitting in the trunk.

Then he could have told me how fabulous I would look driving with the top down in my new convertible, how I wouldn't have to worry about service issues because they'd give me a complimentary loaner car if my car needed repairs, how fun it would be to drive away blasting my favorite songs through a top-of-the-line stereo, and how my golf clubs could fit in the trunk not my skis.

He ended up in the "lucky" category because I already knew what kind of car I wanted before I walked onto the lot. Any salesperson that worked with me would have gotten the sale, regardless of his or her skill level.

I know we've all had luck in our sales and management careers, but would you rather be *lucky* or *skilled*? I want you and your team to be both.

To be a *consistent* Top Performer you need to be skilled, not just lucky.

"It's not what you say, it's how you say it," is so true when it comes to the pitch, and that's one of the main reasons why product dumping is not effective. I once worked with a Top Performer whose face-to-face style with clients was aggressive, cocky, and borderline condescending. He was a product dumper but couldn't see it, even when I pointed out specific examples after his presentation. He had some success because he was talented, educated, and a hard worker, but he never consistently stayed at the top of the ranking report until he learned it was *how* he delivered his pitch, not what he actually said.

Remind your team that it's all about the client—not all about them or your company. This seems simple enough, but it's one common element that far too many salespeople miss.

Old school sales techniques include more product dumping and less product positioning, but as times change, we must also change. The time you spend working on each individuals pitch and helping your team to position your product or service is vital. If they can get the opening and middle of the pitch right, they will find the close becomes much easier.

But Can They Close?

Ah, the *close*—a word that sends a chill up the spine of many salespeople. If someone on your team has a high number of appointments but is closing few sales, it's time to find out why. I'm often surprised at the large number of salespeople who spend hours on pre-sale preparation and on their presentation but don't come out and ask for the business.

Ensure your team is actually asking for the sale.

Many salespeople won't like to admit it, but they are afraid to close, while others tend to ask too early or too often. Others simply "forget." They get so wrapped up in the details of answering client questions, product dumping, or over-pleasing a client that they skip the close and jump right into next steps, also forgetting to soft close along the way to gauge the client's interest. Closing too soon, too often, or not soon enough makes the whole process much more challenging than it needs to be. The good news is that if you do a good job with the pitch, the close will become the natural conclusion to a successful two-way conversation. Here is a checklist to help you determine the effectiveness of your team's interaction with prospects and their pitch.

Check all that apply:

- ❒ Do they do research and know to whom they are selling?
- ❒ Do they truly listen to their prospects?
- ❒ Are they engaging their prospects' senses? (I believe in "Touch It, Feel It, Buy It.")
- ❒ Do they avoid product dumping?
- ❒ Do they ask quality questions?
- ❒ Do they ask enough questions?
- ❒ Do they avoid over-questioning the client?
- ❒ Are they laser-focused during all parts of their pitch?
- ❒ Do they speak in a conversational, non-salesy manner?
- ❒ Are they organized in the way they pitch? Does the pitch flow properly?

If you can place no more than a few checkmarks on this list after you evaluate someone on your team, then it may be time for a pitch makeover. These items aren't "nice to haves." They are "must haves." Without a strong close, each sales presentation or conversation with a prospect is just that—a conversation, not a sale. Turn each meeting with a prospect into a chance to advance or close the sale by using soft closes and learning how to read prospects to determine when to close.

In order to be a Top Performer year after year, your team needs to effectively communicate your company's offering in a powerful and compelling way, which means that you must continually work with your team on how they are presenting and positioning your product. Give them feedback after appointments, engage in role-play, and work as a group to consistently refine their pitch. You can also avoid product dumping by using an outlined or memorized presentation. When you go into a sales meeting knowing exactly what you are going to say, the tendency to travel down product information rabbit holes will drop exponentially.

Every salesperson should have their pitch nailed and be able to clearly deliver the gist of it in a few seconds. If you asked your Top Performers to give you their pitch right now, what would they say? Now think about your Low Performers. If you asked them, what would they say? Chances are, they would struggle to find the right words. Increase your salespeople's closing percentages by helping them refine their pitch so that it is clear, concise, and articulately delivered. This will boost their confidence, help them avoid the temptation to product dump, and increase sales.

KISS: Keep it Simple Salesperson

Sales can be such a complicated monster. That's why it's vital to keep everything *SIMPLE.* Yet many reps have trouble grasping this concept. I've been on countless client appointments where the rep's pitch was so complicated even I was confused—and I worked for the company. They made things seem so difficult that they actually talked a perfect prospect right out of the deal. Clients want simple in an already complex world. They don't want to deal with reps that waste their valuable time by making things more complicated than they need to be.

Instead, coach your reps to stick with benefits that will resonate with the client. What makes your product and service different? What problems does your product or service solve? I'm often amazed at how many salespeople can't directly answer these questions, even though they form the *basis* of the relationship-focused selling that today's customers expect. Keep the sales pitch and the sales process simple, and offer a clear solution to a stated problem. Here are some examples of pitfalls you can help your team avoid so they can keep things simple:

- Don't let salespeople complicate their presentations so much that it causes confusion.
- Let your team know that sales reps that do 90% of the talking don't have high closing percentages.
- Make them aware that it's possible for them to talk so much that the client says "no," just to get them to stop talking. People are busy and they don't want to work with someone who they perceive to be stealing their valuable time.
- Don't PowerPoint clients to boredom (I've witnessed this countless times). Keep slides clean, simple, and

to the point. There's no need for fancy presentations without any real substance.

- Take care not to over utilize material or collateral that complicates the sale, confuses the client, or causes them to tune out. Instead, let them hear from you, the expert, how your offering can help—plain and simple.

Don't try to get fancy. Just help people solve problems. Sometimes it's the simplest things that make the difference between "Yes" and "I'll get back to you." or "Let me think about it."

CUSTOMIZED MOTIVATION

I often get asked, "How can I keep my team motivated?" and I always give the same answer: "You shouldn't have to." Real motivation is intrinsic and any kind of external motivation you provide your team sizzles quickly. It still serves a purpose, but ultimately, nothing you personally do or offer could ever make an unmotivated person eternally motivated—yet some managers try.

You may not be able to do much for people who don't want to be on the team in the first place, but for the team members who do want to be there, you can help them by finding and increasing what truly motivates them to sell more. *True motivators* are those things that motivate each person individually, not the team as a whole. The solution is certainly not what you *think* motivates them, because people are motivated in different ways. What works for one person may not work for another. To identify what truly motivates each person, all you have to do is ask the right questions:

- What's the driving force behind your motivation to excel?
- How do you like to be managed?
- How can I best manage and support you?
- What truly motivates you in life?
- What things can I help you with that would help keep you motivated?

These questions will help you customize your approach so that you can hone in on what works for each individual. When you dig deep, you may actually find that some people want you to hold them accountable for their activity and performance. Others may prefer you leave them alone and let them work. In such cases, you can provide them with some of the motivation they need by giving them more freedom to manage their performance.

Reps don't respond well to being treated like everyone else. You must discover their unique motivations and what makes them tick.

When it comes to motivating and inspiring your team to success, don't just stop with your direct reports. You must have super star folks at all levels of the business that support you. This includes sales support, technical support, customer service, or any other title in your company that plays a part in you and your company being able to win and retain clients.

Behind every top team is top support staff. Without an amazing support staff helping my teams, we wouldn't have been able to stay at the top, year after year. They are the team's right arm and often know more than the team and its leaders. Treat every member of support staff as if he or she is the CEO—and take care of those who take care of you.

When your salespeople and support staff see that you are willing to get to know them on a deeper, more personal level in order to determine what motivates them, this fact itself becomes a motivator. We respond well to those who take a genuine interest in our lives, and we all want to feel valued in our work. So, show your team how much you value them by taking some time to learn the unique motivators of each team member—including everyone that supports you and your team.

Independence Over Co-Dependence

There is a fine line between helping your team and doing everything for them. There is also a fine line between healthy independence and performing as a one-man show too often. Over the years, I've noticed that managers seem to do one or the other: They coddle team members and create a legion of co-dependents or they build a strong, independent team.

Are you creating a Co-Dependent or Independent team?

Managers who do everything for their team breed co-dependence, while managers who encourage a lack of loyalty and cohesion breed far too much independence. I prefer to create independent teams who know I'm there for them and back them when they need me. Your goal is to build a team of people who can do their job without you, sell on their own, know how to resolve issues, and know where to go for help. This also takes you one step closer to building future leaders. When you create independent team members, you are better able to spend your valuable time on larger issues and team strategies. This doesn't put your job at risk; in fact, it only further solidifies your status as an Elite leader.

It's also important to consistently monitor your team's overall attitude toward their job, their lives, the team itself, and the company. Their attitude toward you, their leader, can also make or break their success. When I sensed that a team member did not care for my style, I made it crystal clear I was hired to drive and increase sales. I wasn't hired to be their buddy. They have a right to like or dislike whomever they choose, but pay special attention to when their attitudes shift in order to react proactively, not reactively.

You have the ability to craft the kind of team that fits with your goals and your expectations. And while no two managers or their preferences are alike, in my experience, goals and quotas become more attainable when the team is a unique and cohesive unit of independent salespeople.

It doesn't have to be as extreme as "All for one, one for all," but the team must be able to trust you and each other. Before that trust can develop, it's up to you to:

- Assess their activity to ensure they are being productive rather than busy.
- Give them every opportunity to work in an environment that fosters that productivity.
- Consistently coach to help them improve their pitch.
- Provide individualized encouragement.

All of these things together will help you create independent reps that are motivated to work hard for themselves, for the team, and for the company.

IT'S YOUR TURN

You already know that without your team, there is no need for your job in the first place. So, let's answer some questions about your team and their performance to determine how you can help them continue to help themselves and the rest of the team:

Do you know if your team members are really working? How can you find out? What can you do to ensure they are working?

____

____

____

Do you consistently track team member's activity? Are they doing what's necessary to meet their quotas? If not, how can you help them?

____

____

____

Are any of your team members working in an unproductive environment? If so, what can you do to help them create a better one?

____

____

____

Can you pinpoint why low performance is happening? Is it related to the pitch, lack of training, activity, closing, or a combination?

____

____

____

Does your team tend to collaborate or compete? Is it "every man for himself"? How can you enhance team dynamics and foster collaboration?

____

____

____

Have your team members perfected their pitches? Do they product dump? What can you do to help them improve?

____

____

____

Do you have any team members who are co-dependent? If so, what actions have caused this? What will you do to help them be more independent?

____

____

____

Have you ever had to move a rep up, over, or out? Why? Did you act quickly?

What things do you currently do to motivate your team? Do you feel the techniques are individualized or customized to each individual?

Who's performing over 100%? Is it from one large deal, or many accounts? (I had to terminate someone for low performance despite the fact that in the previous year she over-achieved. The only reason she had performed well was because of one large deal. The following year, she was terminated.)

SECRET 3

IT'S ALL ABOUT THE CULTURE

COMPREHENDING YOUR CULTURE

**"Coming together is the beginning,
keeping together is progress.
Working together is success."**

—Henry Ford

EVERY COMPANY HAS its own unique culture. A company's *culture* is the shared value and practices of the company's leaders and employees. It also includes how its leaders and employees have interpreted, articulated, and incorporated the organization's mission, beliefs, management style, and more into their daily activities and attitudes. Company culture is extremely important because it can make or break your company's reputation and its very future. A company with an adaptive culture that is aligned to their business goals routinely outperforms its competitors.

Before beginning a job at a new company, you may perceive the culture to be one way, but once you're surrounded by it, you discover it's the opposite of what you thought. If some aspects of your company's culture take you by surprise, you could be faced with the possibility of having to adjust your management style to fit the culture. For some, this may be easy. For others, it can be extremely challenging. If you find that the culture doesn't fit your personal brand (and you wish to stay at that company), you must start to identify ways to align your brand with it—even if you don't agree with it on every point.

When it comes to the right culture versus the wrong culture, there is no clear winner in every circumstance; it's all highly situational. The company I worked with for nearly 14 years had a top-down structure—where actions and policies were initiated at the highest level of management. After I had been there several years, they shifted to a bottom-up environment in which ideas and changes were encouraged at every level of the corporate hierarchy. I was in the same role, but the company culture had literally shifted around me. It took some time to get used to, but in the end, both ways worked. This isn't always the case.

The overall structure of your organization doesn't matter nearly as much as your ability to fit in and effectively combine your own team culture seamlessly with the company culture—even if you don't always agree with every decision made by your organization. The key point to keep in mind is this:

Regardless of the company culture, it is possible to drive Elite performance.

Inevitable Shifts in Culture

Companies evolve and change over time. If you've been with your current company for any length of time, you've probably experienced some dramatic shifts in its culture over the years, just as I have. As employees leave the company and replacements are hired, the company will change to varying degrees because each new employee brings their own values and practices to the group.

People are not the only variables that can change company culture. As a company matures to a more established organization and as the environment in which the company operates (the laws, regulations, business climate, etc.) changes, the company culture will also change. These changes may be positive, or negative. Some employees may view them as positive while others may not. As a leader, you must navigate your way through it without causing ill feelings, dissatisfaction, or turnover. The changes in company culture may be intended, but often they are unintended. They may be major changes or minor ones. It's important to be aware of all changes and know how to successfully manage your team through any circumstance.

If you are not sure what the culture is in your company or you want to determine which areas need improvement, the easiest way to assess it is to simply look around. How do the employees act? What do they do on a daily basis? Look for common behaviors and visible symbols. Listen to your employees, your suppliers, and your customers. Pay attention to what is written about your company, in print and online. These will all provide clues as to what your company's culture really is.

Designed to Succeed or to Struggle?

Some company cultures are set up in a way that makes the path to success clearer than in others, and not every culture makes it easy for salespeople to excel. If your company doesn't make it obvious what they expect from you and your team, it's up to you to make expectations more apparent. Additionally, if your company culture tends to place blame on leadership when an initiative fails, that doesn't mean that you have to follow suit. I could have passed the buck on to my leaders for the myriad of issues that stemmed from the multiple reorganizations I experienced and the brutal merger I underwent, but I never shifted responsibility for the successes or failures we experienced onto anyone else's shoulders. The bucked stopped here.

A culture that does not provide equal benchmarks and standards for performance and behavior is not one that is designed to help you succeed. I've been in organizations where

Top Performers were given biased quota increases, assigned additional responsibilities, and expected to make up for Low and Average Performers. In fact, a leader once asked me to tell my Top Performing team that they needed to sell 20% more so the entire region could hit their target. Such treatment can serve as a serious demotivator and build resentment toward you, the company, and other team members.

Regardless of the systems your company culture has put in place for accountability or regarding expectations, you ultimately have to do what's best for you and the people on your team without directly contradicting the culture. Your priority is the success of your team, even when that doesn't seem to be a priority that is intrinsically built into the culture.

If your company changes so much that it no longer aligns with your beliefs, integrity, ethics, values, or more, there is no harm in moving on to one that does align. You as a leader need to use great discernment when communicating. I experienced times with reorganizations when no one in upper management communicated—no one answered the many question asked. They expected the organization to accept all changes with no answers or explanation. Unfortunately, people had families to support and bills to pay, so they required a higher level of communication in order to make sound decisions to stay or leave.

Culture Doesn't Define Performance

Business must always change to keep up with technology, competition, the economy, and many other factors.

Sometimes those changes affect the culture; sometimes they do not. Either way, it's your job to make sure your team successfully handles each decision proactively and with a sense of professionalism. It's also imperative you make clear the company's position on three key issues that directly affect the members of any sales team:

1. **Poaching**. When it comes to poaching territories and clients, such dishonorable acts will always happen, no matter how much you try to stop them. Your team needs answers to important questions like: Does the company allow poaching? Are there rules and boundaries in place to discourage it? Is there is clear plan of action if and when poaching does occur? Regardless of the answers to these questions, it's important to morale that you and other leaders resolve the fallout after someone poaches a piece of territory or accounts and prevent it from happening again. Instill a clear policy to handle poaching issues so if and when they occur they don't get out of control. Here are some suggestions:
    - Communicate early and often with the team that poaching is not acceptable. Don't make them wonder if it's a grey area; make it black and white.
    - Present poaching as a zero tolerance issue. If it happens, let the poacher know that there will be no other warnings. If they poach, there will

be consequences—and you can determine how severe those will be.

- If you have confirmed an act of poaching on your team, address it immediately and make it right to the best of your ability.

2. **Budgets**. Corporate culture can also affect your department's budget. Although they can be disheartening, don't let budget cuts deter your ability to achieve Top Performance. The size of your budget does not determine the extent of your success. You can still post great numbers with a limited budget. I've worked in companies who had both large and small budgets, and at times, they seemed to cut the budget indiscriminately and without warning. In some cases, large budgets can be a distraction. Employees get used to big wallets and looser reins on their spending and often lose sight of what it means to be wise stewards of the company bottom line and client resources.

3. **Entitlement.** It's common for high-performing employees who have been with a company for a long time to develop a sense of entitlement. They can feel entitled to get their way, mistreat or be disrespectful to peers or their leader, freely spend company money, and more. As a leader, keep a keen eye out for this type of behavior and work hard to immediately

squash it. It puts a wedge between employees, serves no purpose, and is detrimental to the workplace.

Regardless of your company's position on these issues, the culture and norms commonly accepted by others in the organization do not limit you or your team in the level of success you can reach. Use the guidelines and regulations that are in place to the best of your ability and focus on what you can do to affect greater success.

Change the Culture or Change to Meet It

When it comes to your team, you want them to work in an environment that gives them the greatest chance for achievement. But sometimes, you may realize that the company culture does not naturally provide that type of environment. Is there anything you can do? Can you change the culture or should you conform to it?

Changing your organizational culture is the toughest task you will ever take on. Your organizational culture was formed over years of interaction between the participants in the organization and changing it can feel like rolling rocks uphill. Before you can change the company culture, you have to decide what you want the company culture to look like in the future. Review your mission, vision, and values and make sure the company culture you are looking to change supports them.

After you have determined what the company culture is, you must align your strategic team goals to match the company goals, if they are not already. Develop a specific action plan that can leverage the good things in your current culture and correct the unaligned areas. Brainstorm improvements in your formal policies and daily practices. Develop models of the desired actions and behaviors. Communicate the new culture to all employees and then over-communicate the new culture and its actions to everyone. Only a company culture that is aligned with your goals—and one that helps you anticipate and adapt to change—will help you achieve Top Performance over the long run.

Principles for Creating an Elite Team Culture

Your team looks to you to learn how to achieve the kind of success you've already been able to achieve. What are you really teaching them? Over the years, I've found there are eight major areas of teaching that every sales leader must implement. These were highly effective for me.

Some of these principles are covered in detail in other sections of the book, but it's helpful to have all eight in one place for quick reference.

1. Create an Entrepreneurial-Minded Culture

I coach my team members to treat their jobs as if they are entrepreneurs instead of employees. When they look at their career from the perspective of a "business owner," it becomes more personal and they subconsciously begin investing more—mentally, emotionally, and physically—in their work. When positioned mentally as an entrepreneur, people take more pride in their territory and in their work, and they understand that they have more freedom to do things their way, as long as their efforts fall within company ethics and integrity standards. You can coach them on making sound financial decisions, giving discounts and pricing that offers the best deal to win the business and help them determine if it would result in a net loss for the company. I consistently had reps almost beg for me to do severe price cuts to win a deal. Yes, we all wanted to win the business but not if it's at a net loss for the company. Help your team think like this. Would they take a net loss on the deal if they owned the company? Where would they cut costs if they owned the company?

Regardless of how compensation is structured—from full salary to 100% commission—salespeople work for themselves. When they are blanketing their territory and accounts, no one can pound the pavement for them, no one else will make their follow-up calls, and no one else will *smile and dial* cheerfully. The team is important, but at the end of the day, your salespeople should learn to foster and grow their business like it's their own. You can help them by showing them how to act like a franchise owner rather than an employee.

2. Create a Culture of Achievement and Excellence

Championship teams don't complain about the last negative prospect and they certainly don't doubt their abilities to get back out there after a loss and win the next game. Make sure the team knows you expect Elite performance at all times from every player on the team. Create a culture where everyone on the team is achieving and over-achieving, not just one or two people. Raise the bar of excellence for all.

3. Create a Culture of Staying True to the Basics

If your team's productivity is slower than it should be, there may be a multitude of reasons. You'll get to the source of the issue much more quickly if you go back to the basics. The best solution is often the simplest solution. Monitor and review their daily, weekly, and monthly activity. Activity leads to sales. Watch their presentations and shadow their calls. Calculate their closing ratios. Have them call a peer to ask where they are off and how they can get back on track. Often times they'll listen to their peers before you. You could tell them the same thing ten times but a peer could say the same time and they'll act as if they heard it for the first time. You can even do some role-playing to figure out where things aren't working in the sales cycle.

4. Create a Culture of Accountability and Responsibility

A successful team is a *responsible* team. Most Top Performers are self-motivated, but even the Michael Jordan of your group needs to be held accountable for his or her actions every now and again. You and the rest of the team are there during those times to remind them why it's important to get back on track. Be cautious of letting Top Performers off the hook just because they're Top Performers. Top Performers should be held to the same standards of accountability and responsibility as others.

5. Create a Culture of Hunting Large Deals—BFD's

My teams consistently ranked at the top because we closed big fabulous deals or BFD's. They are vital to Top Performance as I'm sure you already know. We all want more big deals, those giant, mythical—but hopefully real—deals that make our month, quarter or our year. There is no bigger boost to morale and production than closing a large deal. Encourage your team to hunt for BFD's, but be clear they need to consistently win the small and medium while they're waiting for the big deals to close. Top Performance stems from having accounts of all sizes in your pipeline and not putting your eggs in one big basket. I've witnessed many Top Performers fail because they lost sight of deals that helped them achieve quota until the larger deals closed.

6. Create a Culture of Independence over Co-dependence

Many relationships, both personal and professional, tend to foster co-dependency. It's easy for a co-dependent relationship to develop, so it's your job as the leader to ensure they do not form by encouraging independence. Teach and train your team to avoid calling you for every single issue that pops to the surface. Teach them where and who to go to for answers to specific issues they will face, how to brainstorm their own solutions, and when to come to you with a truly pressing matter. Create an environment where they know mostly to call you for the really important, "it really can't wait" issues. All else can wait for your weekly or bi-weekly one-on-one calls.

7. Create a Culture of Collaboration

Winning sales managers know that collaboration is the only path to long-term success. To me collaboration means working together with peers to share challenges and successes. It also means finding partners to exchange leads and network with. In addition to your leader, develop a list of people your team can contact for advice, mentoring, and to share best practices. Collaborate with these folks instead of competing with them. There's enough business out there for everyone, so work together to achieve more.

8. Create a Culture of Building Networks

There is no doubt that a salesperson can have some success working on his or her own day-in and day-out, but why would you do it alone when you could have access to a support system? Let others carry some of the weight for you and then help them in return. One of your greatest tasks is to encourage networking for more referrals and strategic partnerships. Find others who service and sell to your target client base. Foster and develop relationship with them to exchange leads, get warm introductions to clients and top decision makers. Duplicate your efforts. Building a network means working smarter not harder.

Given the choice between working at a company with a strong company culture that encourages Top Performance and working within a less supportive culture, we'd all choose to work within a strong culture—but that's not always a choice we can make. Whether or not you are working within a culture that brings out the best in people, you have more power than you think to shape and modify that culture to fit the best interests of your team. After all, if it benefits your team, it will benefit the company as well. Regardless whether you get support, encouragement, recognition from your leader is irrelevant. What matters is how you lead and treat your team.

Surviving "Culture Shock"

Having been through multiple reorganizations and a company merger, I have personally experienced culture shock at its best several times. Some of the companies I had worked for changed drastically. Job titles changed, compensation plans drastically changed, territories changed, upper management changed, the leader I reported to changed, some of my team members changed, and the list goes on. These companies had changed so much that the culture shock took its toll on numerous employees. The change was so drastic that many chose to resign. Perhaps you have experienced some level of culture shock in companies you have worked for. If you have, you know how intense it can be and how much it can impact you and your team.

It takes an enormous amount of time and energy to keep your team together during this period of unrest. If this happens to you, or is happening to you, here are a few things you can do to help your team survive corporate culture shock and come out the other side even stronger:

1. **Stay informed.** It is important to be aware of all the changes that are coming so you can successfully manage your team through any circumstance. It's not advisable to act as if it's business as usual. People's lives depend on their job and they need to feel stability instead of fear.
2. **Watch and listen to your team members.** Change can cause your employees anxiety and negatively impact the workplace. They may express their anxiety to you or it may show in their actions. So pay close attention to what they do and what they say and take steps to ease any ill feelings you may detect.
3. **Let them know you care.** Show your team you put their interests first by talking openly and honestly about what's changing, listening to their concerns, and doing whatever you can to help them.
4. **Be a "fixer".** Quickly solve any problems that are within your power to fix. By taking the initiative, you can often "soften the blow" and prevent small problems from growing into big ones.
5. **Keep team members informed.** This is a time to frequently check-in with team members individually and as a group to discuss changes and information as you receive it. When employees know what is coming, it removes some of the anxiety caused by uncertainty.

6. **Make the best of it.** Stay positive and encourage your employees to come up with innovative solutions to challenges created by cultural changes. Remind them of the upsides and unknown possibilities the new changes could present. Remind them they are good at what they do and they will get through it.
7. **Be realistic**. Know that the future changes may not work for every employee. Some employees will choose to leave on their own accord and work elsewhere. Don't take it personally and know these changes are out of your control.
8. **Hire a coach.** There's no need to go at this alone when there are experts and people like myself that have already experienced severe change—not once but multiple times and know how to successfully manage through it. I was one of the fortune leaders who were able to keep my team fairly intact and continued to post Top Performance through temporary turmoil and you can too with some extra help.

Shifts in company culture, either intended or unintended, are inevitable. By implementing these steps, you can help your team better cope with the shock that comes with them. It's also advisable to work closely with someone who is well-versed and has experienced sizeable culture shock to help coach you and your teams through it. The goal is to continue to retain your staff, keep them focused, and keep them selling in spite of temporary company changes.

POLITICIAN OR REBEL WITH A CAUSE?

"Corporate politics" is a taboo word for many people yet it's ever-present in offices across the globe. In its simplest form, office politics or corporate politics are the strategies that people use to gain an advantage personally or for a cause they support. Differences in opinions and conflicts of interests are often manifested as office politics. It all comes down to the manifestation of human communications and relationships.

It doesn't matter how flat organizational structures continue to become in the future. The fact is that corporate politics are here to stay. A study of 400 U.S. workers from staffing firm Robert Half International says that nearly sixty percent of workers "believe that involvement in office politics is at least somewhat necessary to get ahead. There is at least some degree of politics at play in virtually every organization."[2]

No matter where you go or what company you work for, you'll find yourself swimming in a sea of corporate politics, but there is no need to be leery of politics. Every company has a political machine in place, either operating behind the scenes or overtly running the show. Regardless of how it all operates behind the curtain, the faster you design your own successful team culture to work both with

---

2 Cheryl Conner. "Office Politics: Must You Play? A Handbook For Survival/ Success." Forbes, April 2013.

and around corporate politics, the happier you'll be both professionally and personally. Top Performers are those who have mastered the art of winning in corporate politics.

I never liked playing the game, but with time I learned to sharpen my skills. I always viewed it as a necessary evil that I needed to control, or else it would control me. How did I play corporate politics and thrive? My motto was always:

Keep your head down and do your job.

My mastery of the game was subtle. In fact, most of the time, no one even knew I was playing. I simply let my results speak for themselves. I also practiced a few other subtle techniques and passed them along to my teams. Here are some of the key tactics to consider integrating into your strategy if corporate politics reigns throughout your company:

1. **Remain Neutral**. During flare-ups and conflicts, I remained neutral unless someone on my team was under direct attack. I didn't form alliances with any particular group. Try to remain friendly and professional with all. Avoid being quick to take sides. Gather facts first and set emotions aside.
2. **Be Selective**. I chose my allegiances intentionally and I remained protective of the relationships

I developed. I was also extremely selective about whom I consciously chose to share information with and whom I chose to develop working relationships with.

3. **Practice Selective Avoidance**. Figure out who to avoid and who may be threatened by you for whatever reason. Listen to your intuition and don't be quick to open up or say something that could easily get twisted in translation by those who wish you something less than the best.

4. **Know What Not To Say**. I knew when not to say something, when not to disagree, and how to position my point when I did choose to speak up. Knowing what not to say is sometimes more important than knowing what to say.

5. **Be Authentic**. I showed up as myself and I didn't change my personality or management style to fit whatever corporate or political situation in which I found myself. Yet I've watched others cast votes with peers and upper management to be liked or show an alliance.

6. **Let it go**. Know when to stand firm on a topic and know when to let a losing battle go. Be selective with what you choose to hold strong to.

Rise above Corporate Politics. Encourage others to do the same.

Not only can you use these techniques at work, but you can also carry them over to your personal life. Think of the similarities in how you manage your personal life, family life, and emotional, mental, physical, and spiritual lives. You can more effectively manage each area of your life by following similar guidelines.

How to Master the Art of Politics

When I was surrounded by corporate politics, my goal was to be like a ninja—silent but deadly. While others were squawking and boasting, I remained steady and just posted numbers on the board. My leaders knew they didn't have to worry about me and that if I needed something, I'd ask. I was never naïve enough to think that if I ignored corporate politics it would go away. Instead, I attempted to master it rather than allow myself to become a slave to its power. Here are the guidelines I created and then shared with my teams to ensure that I controlled my involvement in and mastery of the politics around me:

1. **Keep It To Yourself.** If you feel like giving someone a piece of your mind or a nasty email, suppress the

urge. It's just not worth it. You might feel good after getting something off your chest, but most of time, it causes more problems than it solves. People may forgive you for speaking your mind, but they will never forget what you said, so rise above the urge to speak your truth and live to see another day with less drama. Also be mindful of the supposedly innocent things you say in confidence. Most things said in secret are not kept secret. Depending upon whom you tell, sharing a secret is often the fastest way to spread information, so disclose at your own risk.

2. **Keep in Line.** As much as you want to lead, and as much as the company may expect you to lead, there will be times when you may have to follow. Top Producers don't typically like to follow, but it is possible to follow and still be a Top Producer. You can lead your team, but also figure out ways to align the team and yourself with the company culture. It's a simple choice: Choose to follow—as long as it doesn't require you to betray your own integrity or morals—or be branded as someone who's incapable of being managed.

3. **Keep Documentation.** When in doubt, document. Document all conversations with team members. Save all emails. You may need them later even if you don't think you need them now. Keep track of any interaction that involves HR policy, sales

territory, compensation, or other areas that might be misunderstood or used against you or your employee in the future. At some point in your career, you will probably be faced with a difficult person or a troublemaker, making it necessary to keep records just in case the situation escalates. Having accurate records in such instances will be essential to making your case and possibly defending your reputation.

4. **Keep it From Escalating.** Choose to build an environment of trust and communication where you encourage open conversation—but not too open. If a situation is publically escalating, resist the urge to get into an open debate, unless you have valid business justification to stand your ground. Take a firm stance and set expectations with your team that you do not promote open negativity in a group setting.

You must address negativity, document when it happens, and even state specific examples of when a person was negative, what he or she said, and how it impacted others. I had a bad case of negativity with someone on one of my teams. It got so bad that team members came to me to discuss how negative this person had been on team calls, in meetings, in groups, and individually. You must shut down this kind of negativity on your team.

Be a positive change agent. Replace politics with honesty, authenticity, and integrity.

You can break the pattern of feeling forced to plug into corporate politics. Don't actively pursue it and encourage your team to follow suit. Corporate politics is only a negative thing if you allow it to be. Choose to see the politics for what it is and learn how to outsmart it so you can focus on creating your Top Performing team.

Should I Stay or Should I Go?

When it comes to finding the right company for you, it's no different from picking the right partner. Sometimes you don't realize a person is not right for you until you have a few months or even a few years invested. In such cases, why settle? Why not move on, find the right mate, and be happy? The same applies to your job. If you choose to stay in a job or company you don't like, in the long run you'll end up feeling like you've sold your soul.

Elite leaders make a conscious decision to do the best job they can every day, whether they love their job or are actively looking for another one. In the same way you can sense when an employee is on his or her way out, your employees can tell when you aren't "all in." When you mentally check out, it's not fair to your team; so make the decision to stay checked in and be the leader they deserve.

You may not like working where you are, but you can still be a Top Performer. Until you have another position lined up and are ready to hand in your notice, don't just do your job—do a great job to the end. Be an Elite Sales Leader and a Top Performer for as long as you're there. Wouldn't you want your salespeople to do the same?

Ignoring corporate politics and dismissing elements of the company culture you don't agree with won't make it all magically disappear. Elite sales managers are comfortable with decisions that are based on politics and company culture. Embrace the decisions, roll with them, and use them to your advantage—because you need your team to do the same.

Can you accept what is? Even if you can't, hold your head high, your heart strong, and your integrity intact.

IT'S YOUR TURN

Hopefully you are working for an organization you believe in and can stand behind with conviction. If you are unsure, you can either choose to overlook your issues with a company's politics or culture or look for one that you can stand behind. To help guide you in determining the best path to take, answer the following questions:

Does your company culture align with your personal brand? If not, what are some of the areas in which a disparity exists?

____

____

____

Do you feel that your culture is designed to set sales teams up to succeed? If not, what can you do with your own team to overcome this issue?

____

____

____

Does your company culture promote collaboration or competition? How can you tell?

____

____

____

How can you create and implement a more collaborative environment regardless of company culture?

___

___

___

Are quotas and territories set up for individuals to succeed? If not, what can you do to make sure your team feels they are fairly treated?

___

___

___

Are you constantly playing corporate politics? If so, how can you begin to unplug and be a subtle master of the game?

___

___

___

Are others on your team actively playing corporate politics? How can you help them disengage without making enemies?

___

___

___

Are you a positive rebel (who knows when not to speak) or a negative rebel who is in danger of being labeled as unmanageable or uncoachable?

____

____

____

SECRET 4

IT'S ALL ABOUT THE HIRING PROCESS

HOW TO HIRE ELITE PERFORMERS

"The kind of people I look for to fill top management spots are the eager beavers, the mavericks. These are the guys who try to do more than they're expected to do—they always reach."

—Lee Iacocca

A STRONG TEAM is like a strong relationship. When you and your partner have built a relationship based on trust, knowing what strengths each person brings to the table, it just makes life that much sweeter. When you have a team full of the right people, all the time and energy you used to spend worrying about your salespeople can be spent on more useful activities, like growing your team of superstars and posting impressive numbers. When you can trust your team to work anywhere, any time, it's a wonderful feeling. It's also an exhilarating feeling to discover this truth:

If you hire the right people, you shouldn't have to wonder if they're working.

I mastered the art of hiring right by doing what we all do at some point—hiring the wrong candidates. I learned a lot from my mistakes and now you can benefit from those lessons. This chapter will describe the proven hiring method I developed over the years to ensure I hired right and gave my teams the best possible chance for success. This method will help you avoid untold hours of frustration, stay miles ahead of your peers and competition, save thousands of dollars for your company, and grow your own bottom line.

The Power of a Proven Process

Having a consistent, powerful interviewing process is the key to building an Elite team. The wrong candidate may say the right things in the interview or look good on paper, but soon after he or she starts, it becomes obvious that they are not a good fit for the position. Once you onboard the wrong hire, it can potentially be a long, arduous, and expensive journey before the person leaves, so be sure to stay faithful to utilizing a consistent and effective hiring process.

Why do some organizations have such high turnover? Is it because all sales positions intrinsically have excessive resignation rates? That seems to be the case on the surface, but that's not the whole story. The real reasons why high turnover plagues our profession are far more likely to be the following:

- Too many sales leaders simply hire the wrong people for the job. They can be smart and capable people but still be the wrong fit for the job.
- Many leaders are pressured to hire quickly. This can cause costly and irreparable errors. It's worth waiting for the *right* candidate, not just any candidate. You can learn to hire the right way by replacing that mindset with my highly effective process.
- A large percentage of leaders are inexperienced with the hiring and interviewing process and they are never given any formal training on how to run the recruiting side of their business.
- Compensation is a common culprit that causes turnover. Some sales leaders overinflate compensation when interviewing. If candidates are improperly informed about earning potential and discover the pay was verbally inflated, they will move elsewhere.
- Top Performers will look elsewhere when there is a lack of connection between a leader and a

salesperson, such as in the case of a personality clash or lack of support.

- High turnover is also due to broken or inadequate internal processes that exist in areas such as customer service, tech support, billing, and other departments. These departments fail to support the salesperson efforts and customers requirements.

Learning how to hire right is a process, not an easily implemented change. With time and a solid, regimented plan in place, you'll never feel the need to hire another person who "will do." You'll expect excellence and raise the bar on your own hiring standards.

Don't just hire good.
Hire great.

Motivation Versus Experience

Early in my career, I looked exclusively for experience and I wouldn't consider someone without it. Over time, I figured out that *drive* overrides *experience*. In an ideal world, it's great to have both, but that's not always possible. When I have to choose between the two, I'd hire a person with internal drive over someone with experience.

My own track record proves that it's not always the most experienced candidate who is the right fit for the job. I had no experience in either of the industries I entered as a sales leader and yet I successfully built multiple top-producing teams on a national level. I had innate motivation and desire to succeed and I hired other people who had the same drive.

My belief is that you can always teach the necessary skill set, but internal drive and motivation can't be taught. People either have it or they don't. You must look for this in every candidate you interview. Don't just hire a warm body. People with this innate trait will find a way to excel against all odds.

In the battle between Motivation and Experience, Motivation reigns supreme.

It doesn't matter how desperate you are to hit your numbers. In most cases, hiring "just anyone" will backfire on you. If you think that any warm body will help you meet a quota, you are in for an expensive and frustrating awakening. It could take months or years to move that person out of the organization.

If you're having challenges attracting high quality candidates, your issue may be compensation, the company reputation, the product, the leader, a personality clash, or just bad timing. However, if you do have a competitive compensation structure and work for a good company, there is no acceptable excuse for closing your eyes and hiring the first person that walks through the door in order to meet your minimums.

Elite leaders hire long-term team members, not temporary solutions.

Do Top Salespeople Make Top Leaders?

It can also be tempting for many sales leaders to promote Top Performers to become sales managers rather than go for an outside hire. It can be argued that top salespeople make top leaders, but in my experience, some do and some don't. I'll admit that it's a sound idea in theory: They excelled as salespeople, so now they can teach others the "secret sauce" of their success, right? Strangely enough, while some end up doing fantastic, many end up struggling intensely in their new role as leader and coach.

Why? Because managing is not the same as direct selling—not even close. Being a good or great salesperson has nothing to do with being a good or great sales leader. Many Top Performers are shocked and grossly overwhelmed when they move into management. They must learn how to gain a new level of respect from peers with whom they once held an equal title with the same job responsibilities and duties.

This is not always an easy task and often times the newly promoted salesperson is met with an array of challenges and much resistance from their peers. They jump in headfirst, bright-eyed and bushy-tailed, overflowing with their own ideas to implement only to be met with opposition and aloofness from their newly inherited team. If you or someone else is considering the leap from salesperson to sales leader, here are a few key things to bear in mind:

- Realize that they will now need to depend on others to make their compensation unless they are a selling manager.
- They must resolve the issues of an entire team, not just their own.
- They advance from caring about themselves to having to care for a team of eight (or so) to manage, with eight different personalities, needs, and desires to juggle.
- They will be required to perform managerial tasks such as completing reports, creating effective meeting agendas, participating in sales leader calls, inviting guest speakers to calls and meetings, training new recruits, brainstorming new ideas to drive new business, shadowing reps on sales calls, and much more.

- They will also be required to resolve internal company or employee issues as well as external prospect and client issues.

The bottom line is that some people are not meant to be leaders or coaches. Ensure you do adequate due diligence before promoting a Top Performer to management. Dig deep. The good news is that there are many different elements to an Elite Sales Team and there is always room for more Top Performers. You need the best salespeople, the best leaders, and the best support staff. Every person has an important role to fulfill and, as the leader, you can ensure that there are no square pegs in round holes.

THE INTERVIEW PROCESS

For the remainder of this chapter, I will share with you the standardized interview process I have used year after year to consistently hire Top Performers. Feel free to adjust it as necessary to properly fit the nature of the job, your industry, your specific company HR policies, the size of your company, or any other area of your business or company culture.

As we dive in, think about it this way: You will spend more time with your team during the workweek than you will with your family, so don't take the hiring process lightly. Choose wisely so that everyone wins.

Let the Process Begin

Selecting your "work family" is no small task. A large selection pool will give you best odds of finding the Top Performers, so ask for as many quality referrals and recommendations from employees and partners as possible. The operative word here is *quality*. I'd rather have five Top Performers than ten average producers. Deliberately hiring average or low caliber salespeople will cost you time and money in the long run.

Gather all quality referrals from internal employees as well as your HR department. Most of my best hires came from internal employee referrals or from strategic partners. You can also gather quality candidates from external sources such as LinkedIn®, recruiters, and friends.

Next, review your pool of resumes. Look for consistent top performance and the presence of any job-hopping. If the candidate is a job hopper, move on. I've never hired a job hopper and I quickly overlook these resumes. I want someone who values loyalty so I can avoid unnecessary turnover and having to retrain.

After reviewing all qualified resumes and determining the pool of candidates you'd like to interview, move to the preliminary phone interview.

The Phone Interview

Before meeting any candidate face-to-face, schedule an initial sixty-minute phone interview even though you may not need all sixty minutes. This allows you to use your time wisely so you can efficiently weed out any Low to Average Performers. You'll also be able to assess a candidate's phone skills. If a candidate demonstrates poor phone skills, such as interrupting, being unprepared, scattered, sounding unprofessional or inarticulate, that's a huge red flag and I do not move that candidate to the next step of the process. Look for candidates who have rock solid phone skills, such as thinking quick on their feet, exuding a good personality, directly answering your questions, taking the time to ask thoughtful questions, and asking for the job—or at least an in-person interview.

Salespeople must be able to "give good phone."

Here's what to do during your sixty-minute phone interview: Before making any calls, develop a list of specific of interview questions you want to ask each candidate. Depending on the details of the position for which you are hiring, the questions you ask will vary. Use these questions to create a standardized interview sheet that you will use for all interviewees. This interview sheet ensures you'll ask the same questions to each candidate. The interview sheet helps you stay organized and remember each person's unique answers. Type their answers below each question so you can go back and refer to them later. It also allows you to ask each candidate the same questions for fair and unbiased comparison.

Remember that interviewing is a two-way street. While you're deciding if you want to work with a candidate, he or she is deciding if they want work with you. So, once you've asked all of your questions, be sure to allow enough time for the candidate to ask you questions as well. After all, candidates have the right to get all the information they need to make the right decision for them. Beware of candidates who don't ask you questions or who ask you very few questions. This is a red flag. If they don't take the time to prepare questions prior to an interview, it could be a sign they won't ask potential clients questions and arrive to sales calls unprepared.

End the interview by telling candidates what the next steps of the interviewing process are going to be. That way there are no surprises and they don't have to sit by the phone wondering if or when they'll ever hear from you again.

Depending on the size of the candidate pool and the complexity of the position, you may decide to have a second phone interview before moving to the face-to-face portion of the process. Take your time to get it right.

After your phone interview or interviews, there are two overriding intangible qualities to consider as you make your selections for the in-person portion of the process:

1. **Likeability Factor.** Decide whether you personally like the person and can see yourself working with them on a long-term basis based on your phone conversation. Will others on the team and within the

organization like them? Will potential prospects and existing clients like and trust them?

2. **Fit Factor.** Determine whether the candidate is a fit based on enthusiasm, motivation, personality, questions the candidate asked, their knowledge of the job, and other considerations that matter to you and the position.

If you sense the candidate is a good fit, do not schedule the in-person interview on the spot. That will give your cards away too quickly, not to mention you may change your mind after speaking with other candidates. Instead, calmly and professionally tell potentials that you still have more candidates to interview and that you or someone else in the company will get back to them if they are selected to move to the next step.

Take note if candidates follow up with a thank you of some kind. Even if I initially love a candidate during the phone interview, I am easily put off by a lack of follow up. A simple thank you email would suffice. A handwritten note or phone call is even more impressive. If they thank you after their interview, odds are they'll make the effort to thank their clients after a meeting. If I like two candidates equally and one sends a thank you note, email, or calls but the other one doesn't, I will typically choose the one that sends an email, note, or calls. I want someone who knows follow-up etiquette and someone who goes the extra mile. They'll likely do the same with clients and prospects.

Top Performers innately do the little things that set them apart and make them shine.

After Phone Interviews

After all of your phone interviews are complete, you have reviewed each candidate's answers to the standardized questions, and you have weighed in on the two-part likeability and fit factors, it's time to decide who qualifies to go to the next step. Schedule an in-person interview with your top two to three candidates. Send the date, time, and location of their interview.

Schedule ninety-minute interviews because one hour is usually not enough time to uncover all the things you truly need to know. Be sure to tell candidates that you will be meeting for the full hour and a half. Ninety minutes is *nothing* compared to months or years spent dealing with the wrong hire.

When scheduling the face-to-face interview, request all candidates bring a written 90-Day Plan that spells out what they will do during their first three months on the job. Let them know that they will be presenting this plan to you during their in-person interview.

Requesting a 90-Day Plan is vital to your hiring success.

You will be able to weed out many candidates solely by looking at their plans. The 90-day Plans they present will be very telling for you. The plans will reveal how they think, write, and present, and whether they really want the job. You can tell if they prepared well ahead of time, or if it looks like they compiled it at the last minute. If they put little to no time or thought into their presentation, it will be painfully obvious. Does the plan actually show activity relevant to the job they're interviewing for? If the plan is filled with typos and other formatting errors, take note of such warning signs. If too many of these red flags are present, they are probably not the right candidates for you—and that's okay. Like dating, it's better to find out in the beginning before you've invested tons of time, effort, and emotion into the working relationship.

The In-Person Interviews

Now it's time to move to the face-to-face interview where you discover what you really need to know in order to make the most informed decision possible. It's important to ask every candidate the same list of questions so that you have a non-biased means of comparison. These questions should be more in-depth than the ones you asked during the phone interviews.

Take time to probe and ask questions about the candidate's past sales performance. Many hiring managers don't do this. They take resumes and answers at face value without digging deeper. Resumes and canned responses will not tell you the whole story. You have to search for the answers you need. Here are ten of my favorite questions to ask about past performance: You may have others you use:

- How did you achieve the performance listed here on your resume (ask about specific numbers if they are given)?
- How long is your typical sales cycle? At what point do you ask for the close?
- What was the average size of the deals you close? (Note if it is larger, smaller, or typical for your company/industry.)
- What is your monthly or quarterly quota? How often did you exceed it?
- How did you achieve top results? Was it with one large deal or smaller deals?
- Tell me about your largest sale. Who was involved, and how long did it take to close?
- How many clients do you manage right now, and what is your follow-up schedule to ensure client retention?

- If I called your current manager, what would he or she say about you?
- What things would your manager say are your strengths and what areas need work?
- What do you personally feel are your greatest strengths and what areas need work?

These questions are excellent ways to break through the fluff and the inflated numbers. It's easy to throw some percentages on a resume. It's hard to back them up with proof. If candidates flounder or find it difficult to back their results it's usually obvious in the interview, so it's best you discover this upfront.

The only way to separate fluff from fact is to probe.

While candidates are answering your well planned, targeted questions, you will have an opportunity to observe many things. Taken together, both their verbal and nonverbal responses can tell you most of what you need to know to make a decision.

There are some specific characteristics to look for during this phase of the interview process that will become valuable indicators of the types of team members they will likely be:

- **Listening Skills.** The gift of gab is an important trait for salespeople, but not at the expense of the skill of listening. Candidates who are talkers are more likely to become product dumpers. Talkers product dump. Listeners sell. Did the candidate actually hear and specifically answer your questions during the interview? I have interviewed candidates who never answered my actual questions. They gave answers that made it painfully obvious they were not really listening; they were just waiting for their turn to talk. I have even asked them the same question multiple times in different ways. Perhaps it's nerves and you should cut them some slack in such cases. However, does that mean they'll have a similar case of nerves in front of prospects and clients?
- **Client Appeal**. How will clients respond to these candidates? Will prospective clients like them, trust them, and most importantly, buy from them? To determine this, listen to how they speak (tone, volume, pace, etc.) and then notice their facial expressions while you are speaking. I worked with someone who frequently had an odd look on his face when listening to a client. His eyebrows squinted together, his head tilted to one side, and his mouth cinched in a strange way. He was completely unaware of his facial expressions, and yet they were the first things that the client and I noticed. Of course, it

was my responsibility to make him aware of these distracting expressions. He had no idea he was doing this and he had done it for so long unconsciously that it was a hard habit for him to break—but he appreciated that I made him aware of it.

- **Cheese Factor.** Salespeople have been trying to break through the plaid jacketed, cheesy salesman stereotype for decades. Selling is a highly skilled profession, so do your part by making sure that you hire consummate professionals, not candidates who have canned, slick answers that would put off potential clients.
- **Evasive Maneuvers.** When you ask a question, do candidates try to avoid or get around certain questions? Your clients demand honesty and straight shooting, so eliminate those who employ evasive maneuvers to skirt around the questions they can't or don't want to answer. I had several candidates that I felt were dishonest with their answers and inflated their experience and qualifications. It's been known that some even falsify the information they put on their resumes and the information they share in their interviews. It's your job to make sure you aren't getting duped.

Once you finish your questions, have candidates present their 90-Day Plans to you as you listen and watch for red flags. Some of the things to notice are presentation design and overall appeal, grammar, clarity, professionalism, and polish. Pretend you are a client and imagine how you would feel about this salesperson if this plan were a sales proposal. Would you buy from them?

After they finish detailing their plan, now have candidates present their sales pitch for the product they *currently* sell, not for your product or service. This is a critical aspect of the interview—it will reveal their selling style and whether or not they engage in consultative selling. You can also see if they product dump, ask good questions, listen, and attempt to close. Once they have presented their plan, thank them, ask if they have any questions, and inform them of the relevant next steps.

IT'S DECISION-MAKING TIME

Candidates are supposed to put their best foot forward during interviews. It's supposed to be a time when they are on their A-game. If they are not, and if "half-prepared" is their A-game, that's likely to be an indication of future performance. Life is too short to hire mediocrity and your career and reputation as an Elite Sales Leader are too important to hire someone who you know, deep down, is not the right person for the job. That is why it's vital to get other people you trust to weigh in on the hire by meeting with the candidates and then sharing their opinions and feedback with you.

If their A-Game is your C-Game, then they aren't the players for you.

Once you have selected your top two or three candidates, have one or more of your peers interview them. Candidates may say different things to someone who they won't be reporting to directly. Encourage your peers to ask specific questions about performance and dig deeper on any topics you missed or on those that need elaboration. A trusted peer may be able to pull additional valuable information from candidates that didn't come out when they spoke with you.

If possible, I highly suggest your final candidates also talk with one or two Top Performers on your team. After each interview is complete, compare notes to see if anyone noticed a red flag that you didn't. I once interviewed a candidate that a peer of mine was considering. After a little digging, I discovered that the candidate did not want to work in the territory he was interviewing for and was hoping to move to a different part of the state. I shared this with the hiring manager, but she still hired the candidate. Sure enough, after six months or so, the new hire's performance was mediocre and the manager was getting close to putting her on a performance plan.

Ask your peers for their opinions, and listen to what they have to say.

For critical hiring decisions, you may want to consider coordinating a group interview where a number of salespeople and/or leaders interview the candidate simultaneously. Each person takes turns asking the candidate planned questions. This will provide additional insight into your candidate, such as how well they can present to a group of strangers and how well they can think on their feet. These are things they will have to do during their career, so why not find out now whether or not they can handle it in an interview process.

Barometers for Successful Hiring

After the in-person interviews, decide whether candidates are going to fit with your team dynamics, represent your company and brand well, and be coachable. Some people may be able to fool you, but after spending sixty minutes on the phone and ninety minutes in person, conducting peer interviews, and hearing both their 90-Day Plan and their pitch, it should be fairly obvious who has what it takes. If you are still unsure, there are a few other minor but important clues you can use to help you decide:

- **Did They Prepare?** Were they fully prepared for the interview? The 90-Day Plan will give you great insight into the level of effort they will give to their job. Did they bring a hard copy of their resume to the in-person interview? If they didn't, you have to wonder if they will forget to pack important documents and materials for client meetings.

- **Did They Close YOU?** After the final question has been asked, did candidates come out and authentically *ask* you for the job? They are being interviewed for a position in sales and Top Producers know that the interview is their chance to sell *you* on *them*, which means at some point, they better go for the close. Did they say with conviction they truly want the position? If they don't ask you for the position, will they ask the client for the sale? In my experience, the answer to that question is usually "No." It's typical they'll ask what the next steps are or what the expected start date is, but do they ask for the job? I am still often surprised at how few actually do.
- **Did They Follow Up?** Just as you did with the phone interview, notice whether they send you a follow up email or note, or if they call you to thank you for your time and for the opportunity. If they don't follow up with you, there's a good chance they won't follow up with clients. Look for these patterns.
- **Did They Provide References?** Asking for references is a mere formality for many hiring managers, but it

> shouldn't be. Ask candidates to bring their references with them to the interview and take the time to call every reference. It's worth it. Calling references is standard, yet I'm shocked at the number of sales leaders who don't make the calls. I've received references with phone numbers no longer in service and people who never return my inquiry call. It makes me wonder why the candidate chose to list these as references.

When you make the final hiring decision, treat candidates the way you would want to be treated. In other words, don't play games with them by dragging out the process or telling them you "don't know anything yet." These tactics make you look inconsiderate, and worse, they could make your top choice accept a job somewhere else.

Top Performers always over-prepare.

Take your time during the entire process. You can even conduct additional phone or in-person interviews if you'd like. There is no set number of interviews that work in every situation. Meet with candidates again and ask different questions. It's like choosing the right partner, so take the time and do your due diligence to choose wisely.

It's okay to go on several dates before you get married.

Learning how to staff the right candidates takes time and practice. Remember, your new recruits will either have it or they won't. You have to ask the tough questions and consistently follow the same standardized hiring process to locate the ones who shine. Now that you know some of my methods for hiring right, you can implement an effective interviewing process to find Top Performers for your Elite Sales Team. Be sure to add, change, or delete any steps to fit your personal style, company, culture, or industry.

IT'S YOUR TURN

Review your current interviewing process to determine if it's highly effective or if implementing a few key changes to the process may be beneficial. Here are the most important questions to ask based on the chapter:

Do you value motivation or experience when it comes to interviewing candidates? Do you feel this has worked for you? Why or why not?

____

____

____

What kind of red flags have you noticed during past interviews? Did you ignore them, address them, or simply eliminate that candidate?

____

____

____

Do you have a specific list of interviewing questions to use for phone and in-person interviewing? Is the list readily available for all to find? Are they actually using it?

____

____

____

What is one question you could ask about performance to identify a potential Top Performer?

____

____

____

How can you avoid being fooled by fluff answers or a padded resume?

____

____

____

Think about the last candidate you interviewed: What did his or her speaking or presentation style imply about how he or she will interact with clients?

____

____

____

Did the last person you interviewed follow up with a phone call, email, or thank you note? If so, what did the language, grammar, and/or writing reveal?

___

___

___

SECRET 5

IT'S ALL ABOUT THE COMMUNICATION

THE DIRECT APPROACH TO COMMUNICATION

"You can have brilliant ideas, but if you can't get them across, your ideas won't get you anywhere."

—Lee Iacocca

COMMUNICATION IS THE basis for all productivity and relationships in the corporate world, and in all aspects of life. It's a powerful force—the manner in which you choose to communicate can make or break your team performance, inspire or deflate moral, motivate or discourage, and save or waste another person's time.

You must be able to clearly communicate if you're going to be an Elite Sales Leaders. How you *think* you are communicating can be drastically different from how your team actually *hears* you. Do you communicate clearly and directly so that your intended message is what comes across?

That's a tough question to answer because we really don't always know how our messages are received. That is why clear and direct communication begins with your delivery method. In other words:

It's not *what* you say.
It's *how* you say it.

It's a leader's job to handle behavior, attitude, and performance issues, put out fires, and make sure the team has everything they need to succeed, all while being a cheerleader, disciplinarian, and coach. How can you communicate all of those seemingly conflicting messages? How can you be firm but understanding? How can you correct bad behavior while encouraging good behavior?

Be direct in a heartfelt way.

We have a choice in the words, tone, and delivery methods we use. Yet people seem to have an overwhelming amount of difficulty saying what they really mean. They seem unable to get their point across effectively in a heartfelt way that best suits the person or people receiving it. In this chapter, we will discuss why communication can be so challenging and examine which elements of communication I have found over the years to play the biggest role in fostering or hindering an Elite Sales Team.

Choosing how you will deliver a message isn't about using gimmicks. I don't have a "five-step strategy" for firing someone or a "six-part plan" for camouflaging negative feedback. When you try to get elaborate with communication and use bullet point tactics that you read in a book or heard in a conflict resolution seminar, things tend to get even messier. Being direct in a heartfelt way is simple—and simple works.

Shoot Straight

Many times, leaders sugarcoat, spin the truth, or use evasive communication—intentionally or unintentionally. These extreme approaches to management will not land you among the Elite. To be an Elite Sales Leader, the fewer gimmicks you use the better. Just speak your mind, with their best interest at heart, and say what you need to say calmly, clearly, professionally, and politely. It really is that simple. It isn't always easy, but it is that straightforward.

My style has always been to shoot straight and speak in a direct manner with my teams. No one has to decode my messages or decipher my real meaning. I simply spell it out in the clearest terms possible. Shooting straight means speaking with professional honesty, an open heart, and without beating around the bush. You have a valid point or comment to make—and you make it. Many team members have thanked me for shooting straight with them over the years. They may not have always liked what I had to say, but they appreciated the honesty and the way in which I delivered it.

You are in the people business and where there are people, there is conflict. It can come from almost anywhere and anyone—and some of the time, it won't go the way you wish it would. You may have to deliver a piece of news that paints you as the enemy. This can be easy for some but a real challenge for others. Being upfront and candid in a non-threatening way is better than leaving your team wondering who's really to blame.

I don't ever want people to doubt my information, intentions, or instructions, so I communicate without ambiguity or secret agendas. However, some leaders don't feel comfortable being direct. I see this sort of discomfort often. The majority of people do not like what they perceive to be confrontation. They think they'll somehow make it go away by not addressing it. I have had peers call me to discuss a problem they are facing, and when I ask, "Have you talked to the other person about this?" quite often the response is, "No." How can you fix something if you can't address it? Of course, you could always sweep things under the rug, but the problem is that after awhile, that rug will have a pretty noticeable bulge.

The sandwich technique is another tactic leaders use to avoid confrontation. This technique involves starting with a compliment and ending with a compliment, but sandwiching a complaint or criticism in between. It's been so overused that people can see it coming a mile away. Retire this technique and just be authentic and real. You'll find that to be far more effective.

Key Communication Questions

We communicate on numerous levels, including on a subconscious level. Our eyes and ears pick up on subtle cues that others may not be intentionally giving us and we form opinions based on those cues without knowing it. Your facial expressions, gestures, and the tone of your voice speak just as loudly, and sometimes even louder, than your words. It's important that you be conscious of the many different ways you communicate, both verbally and non-verbally, and take an active, present, and mindful role in continually improving how you communicate with others.

Before you can improve how you communicate, you have to understand your communication style and preferences. To determine those, ask yourself these questions:

WHO?

Who are you communicating to? Always know your audience. Is it a group, an individual, internal employees, your leader, or external clients? The words you communicate and the message you deliver is dependent on who you are talking to. There may be times when a firm, direct approach is required and there may be times when a softer, indirect approach is more effective. Be mindful that the people you are communicating with may need a different style of communication from you. Be flexible enough to know how and when to tailor your communication style. One size may not fit all.

WHAT?

What are you communicating? Are you a "no-filter" kind of person who says or emails everything that is on your mind? If so, it might be time to start filtering. Not everything that comes to our minds should be said aloud or sent via email. By saying or writing too much, or the wrong thing, it's possible to give the impression that you can't be trusted with confidential or sensitive information. It also gives the impression that you're highly emotional. If you struggle with this, pause for a few seconds to give your brain enough time to decide if what it's about to have you say or write really needs to be said. You don't want to cause irreparable damage.

WHEN?

When do you communicate? Do you send emails and texts at all hours of the day and night? If so, what sort of subliminal message does this send to your team? Do you send or check messages during meetings? If you do, be prepared for your team to do the same. Set clear boundaries for yourself and your team. Start thinking about when you communicate and ensure it's not done in a way that disrupts team members' productivity or teaches them that emailing at 3 a.m. is the norm.

WHERE?

Where you communicate with your team members can really matter to them. Depending on the type of information, the right place may be the office if you have one. Maybe it's minor enough to discuss over the phone. Perhaps the conversation warrants some private, one-on-one time over lunch. Of course, if you're working in a virtual environment, you'll have no choice than to communicate by phone unless you use camera, Skype, or video. There are certainly places where an important discussion with a rep must never take place—in front of a client or in a group setting.

WHY?

Why are you choosing to communicate with this person or group? Determine what your clear intention is for the messages you deliver. Keep it simple and direct. Sometimes, simply asking this question allows you to get to the real meaning behind your own words and allows you to deliver your message in a clearer, more concise manner.

HOW?

Have you thought about how your tone is perceived, not just verbally, but also by email, phone, text, and during one-on-one calls? There is a preferable tone for every occasion. In electronic communication and even over the phone, tone plays an instrumental role in conveying your emotions and intent. If you are not sure how you sound to others in emails or over the phone, record yourself or ask colleagues to give you an honest assessment of your tone. You may be surprised by what they have to say. Keep it factual, non-emotional and allow the recipient to talk.

Asking yourself these questions will help you become more aware of how you are communicating with others. Keep what you've discovered top of mind before writing an email, meeting a new prospect, sending a text, calling a rep, conducting a one-on-one meeting, or interviewing a new recruit. Your careful consideration of these elements of your communication style and preferences will determine if your team will listen to you and follow you. Elaborate, stern, rambling, bullying, envious, and overly complex communication won't work. Scare tactics won't work. Being unresponsive doesn't work either. What you need to practice is direct, heartfelt, conscious communication.

Accepting What Is

Personality issues abound in the people business. If someone doesn't like you, there is really not much you can do about it. As long as they are on your team, however, there is one thing that you can make crystal clear. You don't all have to go for drinks after work or even like each other, but everyone is expected to achieve or exceed their targets and treat others with respect. Period.

Part of being direct, setting expectations, and shooting straight is learning to accept the team that you have. If you have consistent Low Performers or people with negative attitudes on your team, you can always do something about it. But once you've set the wheels in motion, the situation won't resolve itself overnight. In some cases, you have to work with the cards you were dealt—until and if you can replace them—particularly if you inherit employees you did not directly hire.

There have been times in my career when personality or performance conditions with team members were not ideal. I knew I couldn't sit on my hands or close my eyes until the issue miraculously disappeared. Instead of spending valuable time and energy wishing something away, accept the team you have and do the best with each of them despite of personality issues. You need to be accepting, but that doesn't mean you have to put up with dysfunctional behaviors when there are ways you can fix it. The following are some of the more damaging personality issues you may come across and a few ways to help with each:

- **Arrogance.** Dealing with arrogant people takes a lot of patience and a great deal of self-control. When someone on your team is displaying arrogant, narcissistic tendencies, you may decide to allow it to go unchecked as long as it's not affecting other team members. But if their behavior is unacceptable, inform the offender that his or her attitude will not be tolerated. While it's unlikely that your company has any defined rules or regulations in place that focus solely on egotism, anyone who has dealt with behaviors such as arrogance, stubbornness, and resistance, knows it can be a huge disruption to the workplace. If it escalates, make it clear that this person's attitude and behavior have become problematic and interfere with others who are trying to do their duties. Be sure to point out specific instances when this has occurred. And don't forget to document these conversations.

- **Extreme Posturing.** You know there are unhealthy levels of posturing within your group when you sense disdain between coworkers and witness petty posturing. You may notice your people exaggerating their accomplishments and pretending to have a frantic pace in an attempt to portray themselves as busy rising stars. Instead of catering to them, focus on helping others and over-delivering. At the end of the day, business results and performance are the only real sources of credibility in sales. Coach each individual and make everyone aware that this behavior could negatively impact their personal brand and may cause co-workers to separate from and avoid them.
- **Irritability.** Unnecessary short fuses reduce or prevent the flow of information and teamwork. This type of animosity is a barrier to people doing their jobs. If someone does you wrong, take it up with that particular person first. Do not take it out

on everyone else or lash out at people who need information from you. When principles are not at stake, be a pleasure to work with. Help your team understand the goal is for all employees to foster a positive, supportive, and collaborative environment. No one wants to work with cranky people.

- **Fakeness.** Being authentic is an important basis of effective leadership. People want to know that you say what you mean and you mean what you say. In the sales world, certain people will always have hidden agendas and motivations. While good friendships will help the workplace be more enjoyable, you must also be discerning in choosing your friends. As George Washington said, "Be courteous to all, but intimate with few, and let those few be well tried before you give them your confidence."
- **Procrastination.** Procrastination is a symptom of overconfidence, apathy, or lack of focus. Complacency lowers your personal productivity and the productivity of your team. To avoid its grasp, set deadlines and enforce them. Typically it seems there are one to two people on every team who are late to respond, tardy submitting reports, late to calls, etc. Address these promptly. Professionally and politely state they need to participate and be on time, then ask how you can help them do so.

- **Sabotage.** A saboteur takes competitiveness to a truly dysfunctional level. Whatever their reasons for their attempted subversion, saboteurs tend to be highly selfish individuals. There isn't much you can do to protect yourself from their scheming behaviors, except to keep your radar on high alert and to be extremely cautious of them. There could be several reasons why they feel the need to sabotage others. The saboteur only hurts himself. Don't be one and don't allow one on your team.
- **Backstabbing.** Employees who backstab coworkers create a culture of paranoia that is a detriment to your team's productivity and morale. Backstabbers are the kind of people who will overtly do things to undermine, embarrass, or place leaders and co-workers in potentially career-damaging situations. Backstabbing can include everything from talking trash about someone behind their back to taking credit for another's successes. Backstabbers feel the need to attack others because they are overly ambitious and, on some level, insecure. Deterring backstabbers begins by creating a team culture with clear rules of accepted behavior and conduct, then enforcing accountability. It's best to address issues of backstabbing as soon as possible. Have a frank discussion with offenders about what is permissible and what is unacceptable and clarify the consequences they'll face if they fail to comply.

- **Negativity.** Some people always see the glass as half empty. Even if you are in the middle of praising them for a big win, they'll find a way to turn it into a negative. I once had a chronically negative rep on my team. Other reps would proactively complain to me about this person. As the leader, I knew this behavior had to be addressed. Believe it or not, some negative people do not even realize they are being negative. Bring their negative behavior to their attention, clearly state the example of their negativity, and explain why that attitude is damaging, how it is impacting your team, and that it must end.
- **Ulterior Motives.** If you say that someone has an ulterior motive for doing something, you believe that they have a hidden reason for doing it. This type of employee can be poisonous to the rest of the team because neither you nor the rest of the team can trust anything he or she says. I have worked with a multitude of personalities and many had ulterior agendas. They did or said things that painted them in the best possible light in front of the boss, such as taking someone else's idea and making it sound as if it was theirs. They alter the details of a conversation to make themselves look better than the reality. These people are also known as manipulators. If they have problems on their team, they spin the truth and lead the boss to believe their team loves them. When it comes to these individuals, base your management

of them on their numbers and other tangible factors since you can't rely on their words.

You can't avoid these types of people in the workplace, especially when you are their leader or peer. But you do have options. One option is to find a way to accept them, deal with their behavioral issues in a way that won't permanently damage your relationship with them, and work together in spite of your differences. The other option, if the behavior is severe enough, is to involve HR and your supervisor. I worked with a rep that was utterly rude and disrespectful to me as a leader and had such incomprehensible behavior I had no other choice than to contact HR and write him up for bad behavior. Poor performance isn't the only reason for putting someone on a plan.

Ensure personality issues don't become performance issues.

Although there may be many less than healthy personalities in your workplace, we all possess free will. You can either chose to remove yourself from this type of workplace or to stay and become the best leader you can be by setting a good example for others. The latter is the better choice, albeit the harder one. Small steps in this area result in giant leaps toward healthier work environments. Set the tone and lead the charge to ensure you promote an environment of positive communication.

Communicating with Low and Average Performers

How do you communicate effectively with salespeople who are struggling? It's a question that plagues managers at Fortune 500 companies and start-ups alike. It's difficult to know when to remove underperforming team members. When the channel of communication is opened, it allows you to give sound guidance, encouragement, or training to get them back on track.

Most of us leaders probably feel like a little professional nudge in the right direction is a more economical choice than the time-consuming, expensive, and arduous task of hiring a replacement. I know I'd prefer to give my struggling salespeople a chance to improve and bring their results up to company standards rather than be quick to cut them loose.

So what do I do? Contrary to what you might think, I don't start with them; I start by examining the way I've been communicating with and coaching them up to that point by asking myself questions like:

- How can I improve my communication with them?
- How have they responded to coaching?
- Do they still seem coachable?
- What ways do they typically communicate with their team members and with me (email, text, in-

person, or phone calls)?

- How can their communication be improved?

In short, I determine if there has been a breakdown in communication somewhere along the way. If you don't perform this assessment first, then all the reaching out, coaching, and encouragement you give will likely not be heard.

After the communication assessment is done, take some time to analyze the rep's sales metrics. Use those numbers to create a report that you can use to show where he or she is performing poorly based on FACTS. Then think about all the areas where you believe the rep needs improvement. This way, when you meet with the rep, you'll have specific, metrics-driven goals for them to hit.

Once you've done that, sit down with rep for an open, honest one-on-one conversation. Ask them directly what struggles they are facing. What makes their jobs difficult? What could they do better? What could you, their leader, do to help them improve? Sometimes Low Performers will be very open and will tell you a lot of things. Other times you will have to pry by asking how they're managing their time, what an average day looks like for them, how they run sales calls, and how they follow up.

Let the rep know you truly believe they can achieve higher performance and you want to help them improve. Review their sales metrics together and go through their numbers stat by stat—praising for areas of strength and highlighting areas of opportunity. Finally, outline specific goals you'd like them to work toward over the next few weeks.

Once you've completed these steps, it's time to focus on one-on-one coaching. The emphasis during this phase will be for you to gain agreement on what is said every step of the way. In short, you want to make sure that the rep understands what you are saying and that the two of you stay on the same page. Of course, just as you do with the rest of your team, communicate with them directly without sugarcoating or masking your true intent. Your heartfelt intention is what shines through and what allows them to be open to the coaching.

Elect one or two areas at a time to work on to get better results (activity, pitch, prospecting, closing, etc.). That also means you may have to remove distractions, change the methods of communication to better suit their needs, and give additional management support. With a little patience and a little conscious effort to focus on how to come across and their preferred channels of communication, you can get through to even the most frustrated struggling rep.

If you begin to see improvement, great. Celebrate his or her achievements and coach them on their challenges. If after the designated time period is up you fail to see any significant improvement, you can part ways knowing that you did everything in your power to help them before letting them go.

Communicating with Top Performers

Frequently, sales leaders give their time and attention to Low and Average Performers at the expense of Top Performers.

This is a mistake. Top Performers need your attention just as much, and in some cases more, than Low and Average Performers. But communicating with and managing them can be tricky. Here are a few tips to help you out.

- Determine if they're high or low maintenance: If they're high maintenance, even though they may drive you crazy at times, they're doing a great job for themselves and your team so your job is to help them be even better. Often times Top Performers think they don't have to be responsible and accountable to their leader because they have numbers on the board. I've had situations where they've missed team conference calls, showed up late to meetings, and acted like sitting through a meeting was the most painful thing they've ever done. Be careful. Allowing this type of behavior can cause dissension amongst the team, as well as feelings of resentment and unfair treatment. Yes they may have earned the right, but it's only fair that you hold them accountable as much as the others on your team. If they're low maintenance, they'll let you know when they need you. That doesn't mean you stop all communication and let them run free. You still need to hold them accountable the same as you are the others are but they like being able to enjoy the freedom of "doing their own thing" and you need to be comfortable allowing them this flexibility.
- Show them how to maximize the compensation

program: Top Performers quickly want to know what they need to do to make the highest commissions possible and they're typically highly motivated by money, ego, and success so empower them so give them a lot of encouragement, praise and recognition.

- Don't keep what they're doing a secret: Have them share step-by-step what they do to drive high activity and win new clients so others can duplicate their success.
- Talk with them about their career path. Many Top Performers are working hard because they do want a promotion and they do want to go to the next level with their career. As an Elite Sales Leader, your job is to encourage and develop new leaders.

By following these steps you can keep Top Performers happy and doing what they do best: closing deals.

EFFECTIVE COMMUNICATION IN MEETINGS

We've all been there—the meeting that drags on and on; the meeting where everyone sits fiddling with his or her smartphone; or the meeting where almost everyone in the room is wondering the same thing: Why am I even here?

Meetings fill an increasing number of hours in the workday and yet many salespeople consider them to be a waste of time. According to a survey of U.S. professionals conducted by Salary.com, meetings ranked as the number one office productivity killer (interestingly, dealing with office politics was a close second).[3]

They may seem like time wasters, but meetings can serve a real purpose in uniting your team and helping them discover how to communicate their ideas in ways that actually get heard. You can run effective meetings that leave your employees feeling energized and excited about their work. The key, of course, is in how you communicate with your team before, during, and after the meetings. Here are some key points:

- Do not have a meeting for the sake of having a meeting. Even if it's been a few weeks since your last meeting or call, only schedule one if you have a legitimate reason that can be easily communicated to the team.
- Respect others by starting and ending on time. I've been on countless conference calls and attended meetings where the person leading the call said, "We'll just give it a few more minutes for people to join the call." That sets a precedent that it's okay to be late. It's also disrespectful to the people who do show up on time. The same applies for ending meetings on time. Just like a delayed flight alters flight times for the rest of the day, if a meeting ends late, it can cause other meeting delays or even cancellations, it can upset clients and prospects, and

3 http://www.salary.com/2013-wasting-time-at-work-survey/slide/13/

it can cause employee dissatisfaction and potential loss of sales and revenues.

- Avoid over-loaded agendas. In fact, pull topics if necessary. Keep the agenda tight and relevant.
- It's not always possible to get 100% participation at every meeting, but that shouldn't stop you from encouraging it. If certain reps are silent, get them to contribute by asking them specific questions that are not too difficult to answer so everyone is accountable for participating.
- Encourage participation. Don't be the only one that talks. The leader of the meeting is also the facilitator. In other words, it's your job to get other people communicating their own thoughts and ideas. Encourage them to share valuable and helpful information with the entire team.
- As you move through the agenda, cover all topics succinctly. It's easy for meetings to go down rabbit holes and eventually veer completely off topic. Don't dwell on any one topic for too long unless it's scheduled as the main agenda item. Stick to the agenda to keep the meeting momentum going.

My successful career and consistent track record of producing flourishing teams have proven that sales won't plummet if you have bi-weekly calls instead of weekly, so long as you've hired right. Regularly communicate to your team and coach your reps to get the help they need when they need it. Weekly one-on-ones and team meetings or conference calls are absolutely necessary if you have something worthy to discuss. If not, I believe you need to just let your people sell.

COMMUNICATING DURING FIRE DRILLS

"Lack of planning on your part does not constitute an emergency on my part." What a true statement that we can all relate to. After all, it's happened to all of us at some point: You are working hard when suddenly the figurative fire alarm goes off. A co-worker, supervisor, or a client needs something immediately. It is an "emergency." Suddenly, everyone on your team is scrambling to address the issue at hand and all other work is halted.

All other priorities get pushed aside. Progress on other work and selling comes to a screeching halt. What would happen if you chose to say no to someone's last minute request? How would you communicate that in a way that won't offend others on the team or cause them to feel you don't value their issues?

It's not easy. But it is possible. Depending upon who sounded the alarm. If it's a client, you absolutely need to respond promptly. If it's upper management, you'll need to comply. The only thing you can really do is have a professional and frank conversation with your leader and ask if there is any way possible to get more advanced notice in the future.

If the alarm was pulled by one of your direct reports,

there's much more you can do to control and manage the situation. Start by initiating a dialogue with the person or people who are asking for help. This is best done face to face, if possible, since email is notorious for misrepresenting tone and intent, especially when it comes to sensitive subjects. Once you open up that dialogue, here are some good questions to figure out as a team:

- Is this truly urgent?
- What impact will it have upon other work?
- What lesson is to be learned from the situation?
- Is there an underlying issue that is causing the situation?
- Does anyone need to be held accountable?

How do you deal with crises in your workplace? Does your team sometimes react and bring things to you that are not truly urgent? If this is an ongoing issue on your team, address it at your next team meeting as a group. Clearly communicate what constitutes a fire drill and what does not. Communicate your expectations about priorities and time management. In the future, here are some phrases you can teach your team to avoid (and remove from your communication as well):

- "I need this now."
- "It is overdue."
- "We have a serious problem."

This type of stress-inducing communication is far too

common in our fast-paced work environments. Many so-called emergencies are not really that important. So when the next one comes up, take a few moments to consider your actions before immediately dropping everything. Before you let one of your colleagues interrupt others' productivity, ensure that the situation is truly warranted.

COMMUNICATING ABOUT COMPENSATION

Can the way you communicate about pay change the way the entire compensation structure is perceived or even utilized by your sales team? Absolutely. Your ability to convey how your team can most effectively maximize the compensation plan (I say "max the comp plan") can make all the difference in giving your salespeople the motivation they need.

When you communicate their plan to them in a way that is transparent and easy to understand, in some cases, it will almost feel like they've just gotten a raise because you've shown them what will put money in their wallet.

Because money drives behavior, ensure each person on your team clearly understands how to maximize his or her compensation plan.

A good place to start is by clearly communicating with your team how their compensation plan works and how they team will be paid. This is critical information for them to know, so take your time crafting your explanations. Use examples and "what-if" calculations to help salespeople understand what they need to do to earn more. Then schedule one-on-one meetings to review the plan with each of your direct reports.

Incentive plans can be complex, particularly in the sales arena. So, simplify them for each team member by walking them through each part of the salary and commission structure. Encourage questions and thoroughly process their responses in order to read between the lines so that you can help them understand the ins and outs of the plan. You'll find your team will become excited about the new potential that has opened up to them by fully understanding what they need to sell to make the most money.

Money plays a key role in motivating salespeople, so it's important that compensation is aligned with your sales strategy to ensure you are coaching your reps to focus on selling the right products or services.

It's also important to correctly align pay with company objectives. This provides a win-win-win outcome for your team, for you, and for the company. If designed and then communicated effectively, your sales compensation plan should achieve the following:

- Align with the organization's goals. Effective plans communicate goals primarily through the selection of performance measures aligned with business objectives.

- Motivate salespeople. Compensation plans motivate salespeople by providing rewards for performance.
- Direct salespeople to the appropriate activities. When your team knows what activities or targets yield the most reward, it helps them prioritize their time appropriately.
- Support team efforts. When appropriate, effective plans ensure that team efforts are appropriately rewarded and receive a level of focus that aligns multiple reps' efforts with the company's business objectives.
- Recognize superior performers. Effectively communicated enable recognition of Top Performers, which reinforces successful sales efforts in a nonverbal, but powerful way.

DIRECTLY COMMUNCATING CHANGE

Businesses will always change, as will your organization. It is inevitable. So, how do you rate as someone who embraces change and leads change in an organization? Having survived multiple reorganizations (many that were only six months apart) and a complex company merger, I understand how challenging it can be. At some points during these changes, communication was stellar. At other times, it failed miserably.

The reasons why the changes failed at times generally had little to do with the change itself. Most of the time, the change simply wasn't communicated properly. When it comes to change, you have to give people the necessary time to adjust to a new idea because people resist change. That's just the way most of us are wired. When leaders spring a sudden change on employees it causes them to question the entire organization. It also causes people to worry about their job security and begins to erode the trust they have in their leaders and upper management. Change should never be presented as an ultimatum, nor should it be brushed off as "no big deal," especially if those changes directly impact other people's jobs or compensation potential.

At one of my former organizations, they announced they were moving employees from an office environment to a virtual environment with no explanation. It caused a company-wide panic, but once people understood the millions of dollars the company would save and the flexibility they'd have working from home, they fully embraced the idea. People got excited about knowing the company would fully equip them to work from home instead of fearful about the change. In fact, some said they wished the change had been made a long time ago.

Humans are creatures of habit and changes at work can shake us out of our comfort zone. People thrive through routine and predictability, which give us a sense of control in a world that is out of our control. When there are big changes in your workplace, your team is suddenly thrown into a state of uncertainty. It can be stressful and bring up a variety of fears, but the extent of that stress and fear has a lot to do with the way change is presented, or not, by management. To help your team more effectively deal with change, here is one key to keep in mind:

Presenting the WHY
helps reduce the fear of the unknown.

Even if employees do not agree, they will at least know *why* a change is being introduced. Take time to explain what the change means to them specifically and how it will impact each person individually. For example, if you are changing the compensation program, tell them WHY. If you explain why, it's perceived as less of a dictatorial move and gives people the ability to understand the reason for the change. If you're moving from an office to a virtual environment, explain why and reassure employees you'll help them through the transition. If you are planning a company reorganization, clearly communicate why you are making the changes.

Most employees respond to internal changes in their work environment with nervousness and resistance because change is associated with negativity for the majority of people. There is no end to the list of changes that could raise the alarm in your team members. Such changes are revised job descriptions or duties, changes to the commission structure, territory changes, hiring freezes, budget cuts, management changes, and more. The most nerve-wracking changes are anything that brings up fears of being unemployed.

When change is successful, it is often because the change is communicated in ways that allows it to be less intimidating and viewed as a positive transformation. Here are some of the ways I've seen change communicated successfully over the years:

- Change should be communicated with honesty and transparency. No one can feel blindsided or surprised. Employees must also be given some time to adjust to the idea.
- The presentation of the change must be done in an authentic manner. It can't feel like you are being sold a bill of goods. You must honestly help everyone see the benefit(s) that could come as a result of the change.
- Leaders should be direct and should not try to spin the truth. This enables others to more readily trust that the change is positive.
- It's also important to avoid talking AT others, as in, "This is how it is. Deal with it." Instead, it needs to be a two-way conversation. The team needs to be able to voice their questions and concerns and you need to be the one to help work them through it.
- Managers and leaders who dedicate a good deal of time to talking about the changes in a real, open manner as a group *and* with each individual

separately will succeed far beyond those who say, "Here it is. You're lucky you still have a job."

- Ask for the teams' openness to the change and help them see it could potentially be a positive.
- Reinforce that things will be okay—as long as it really will. If you don't know what the future holds, reassure you'll help them and you'll get through it as a team and be stronger because of it.
- Quickly squash the naysayers. They have a tendency to plant harmful and distracting seeds in others heads and can negatively impact your entire team. Spend additional time with them and advise them you need their support instead of opposition.

It's perfectly normal and healthy to be a bit fearful, confused, or unsettled by workplace changes at first. It's normal to feel nervous and upset when things go out of our control. The unhealthy part occurs with inappropriate or unhelpful responses on the part of a leader. If you tee up your conversations properly, it helps reduce the number of hours wasted on needless chatting, complaining, and unrest. Your team can quickly move on and get back to selling without worrying about their jobs.

COMMUNICATION BETWEEN GENDERS

Although men and women speak the same language, the way we communicate is very different. As a result, it's easy to misunderstand, misinterpret, or simply not get where the other is coming from. To be an Elite Leader, you must have a solid understanding of these differences so you can effectively motivate, coach, and get along with team members of both sexes. Here are just a few examples of how men and women communicate differently:

- Men tend to speak more concisely while women prefer to elaborate or explain their points of view.
- Men tend to enjoy giving information as a way of demonstrating expertise. Women tend to like sharing information to build relationships.
- Men tend to present their ideas as if they are fact. Women often phrase their ideas as questions and add disclaimers such as "It's just my opinion," or "I may be wrong."
- Men tend to listen to solve problems. Women tend to listen to gain understanding.
- Men tend to make unilateral decisions and are more comfortable giving and taking orders (more so if it's from higher level males). Women tend to seek input and consensus and are more comfortable with giving and taking suggestions from men and women.
- Men tend to argue more and find it interesting to disagree. Women tend more often seek agreement and see disagreement as threatening to a relationship.
- Men tend to not seek help and direction, whereas

women are more likely to ask for and accept help.

- Men tend to engage in verbal bantering and derogatory comments to establish rapport while women tend to feel a certain level of formality is more appropriate.
- Men tend to prefer to receive individual acknowledgement while women tend to be satisfied to be congratulated as part of a team.
- Men tend to be judged as being better at monologue—women tend to be judged as being better at dialogue.
- When a man nods, it generally means he agrees. When a woman nods, it generally means she is listening.
- Men tend to be more logical and women tend to be more emotional.

While this list in not comprehensive, understanding just a few of these differences will enable you to customize how you communicate with different genders, which in turn will make you a more effective leader. When you speak to someone in their own language, you dramatically increase your chances of getting your message across clearly and effectively, without confusion or misinterpretation.

I've dealt with my fair share of issues stemming from gender differences during my career. The vast majority of my male and female salespeople respected me and listened to what I had to say based on my track record, expertise, and the way I communicated with them. In one particular instance, however, it was obvious that a male rep did not enjoy working with me and he made it clear from the start that he didn't appreciate reporting to a female leader.

He made my job as his leader a genuine challenge by resisting all coaching and feedback. Although he was new, he told others who had been with the company for years how to do their jobs. To make matters worse, he spoke in a condescending tone and enjoyed getting his daily jabs in by constantly referring to me as "boss." He'd say, "Hey boss.""What's up boss?" "What do you want to talk about today, boss?" Pretty soon communication had all but degraded between us.

Even though he was new to the company, product, processes, and pricing, he acted as though he knew everything. He regularly told everyone (including me) how intelligent and "right" he was. Fellow teammates would regularly come to me to complain about their lack of patience for his arrogance. As his leader, I knew I had to address it, especially since his peers were struggling with his behaviors as well.

If you can relate to this story to any degree, then you probably had the same choices to make as I did. You can choose, like I did, to let a lot of the little things go and make a decision to focus and coach on the biggest issues. I decided to start by having a conversation about how "arrogant" his brand was becoming. I also told him that I observed him behaving in the same arrogant way in front of clients and prospects, so much so that many clients were no longer willing to work with him.

I knew that this rep did not want to hear any of this from me, but I believe that everyone on my team, regardless of gender, must be respectful of fellow team members, their leader, and clients. If he wanted to disrespect me, that was one thing. But he wasn't going to spread that disrespect around. If the rep wasn't okay with my open, honest feedback, he had the option and the freedom to work elsewhere. Plenty of male reps were thriving on my team. For that reason I knew that this was a case-specific issue, not an indication of my inability to communicate with him.

I communicated to *all* members of my team, including the resistant rep, my guidelines about what I expected from them—and I gave them autonomy to figure out their own way of getting there. This goes back to the idea of Individualized Management. You have to find what works for each member of your team based on individual preferences.

Customize your communication for different personalities and social styles.

This mindset is vital for future success. Elite Leaders don't let little things like gender differences get in the way of effective communication. Elite Leaders are capable of working with all personality types. What matters most is how that manager communicates with each member of his or her team. You have to work together anyway, so why not make the most out of every situation?

We're in a high impact people business and it's a given that not everyone you work with and interact with will always see eye to eye on key issues. In fact, it's extremely rare when they do. In the end, the only thing you can control is your own communication. You can ensure that it is direct, honest, and unbiased. The way you communicate can and should be universal across the many types of salespeople you manage—and by communicating in a heartfelt, sincere way, you can teach others how to do the same.

Always be aware of what you say and how you say it.

IT'S YOUR TURN

Communication is something you must focus on daily, both in your work and personal life. It may take a lifetime to master, but you can start moving in the right direction today. To get you started, here are some questions about the current state of the communication within your team:

If each person who reported to you were asked to rate you on a scale of 1 to 10 on how clear and direct your communication is, what average rating do you think you'd get? Why do you think that?

If you could improve one thing about the way you communicate, what would it be, and how would that impact your team?

Do you individualize the way you communicate, or do you employ the same methods for the entire team?

____

____

____

How would customized communication impact the results for each individual?

____

____

____

Who should you contact in your organization for issues with customer service, technology, IT, marketing, pricing, contracts, and more? Do you have the names written down in a database that your team can access?

____

____

____

Have you recently experienced any major changes in your organization? If so, did you take the time to clearly explain to your team why the changes were happening? What else can you do to help them deal with change?

____

____

____

Do you ever have difficulty communicating with team members of the opposite sex? What can you do avoid confusion and ensure understanding?

____

____

____

How well do you communicate with team members who are struggling? What steps can you take to help them? What do you do if you determine they are uncoachable?

____

____

____

How many meetings do you have each week? How many SHOULD you be having? Do you have too many or not enough?

____

____

____

SECRET 6

IT'S ALL ABOUT THE RESULTS

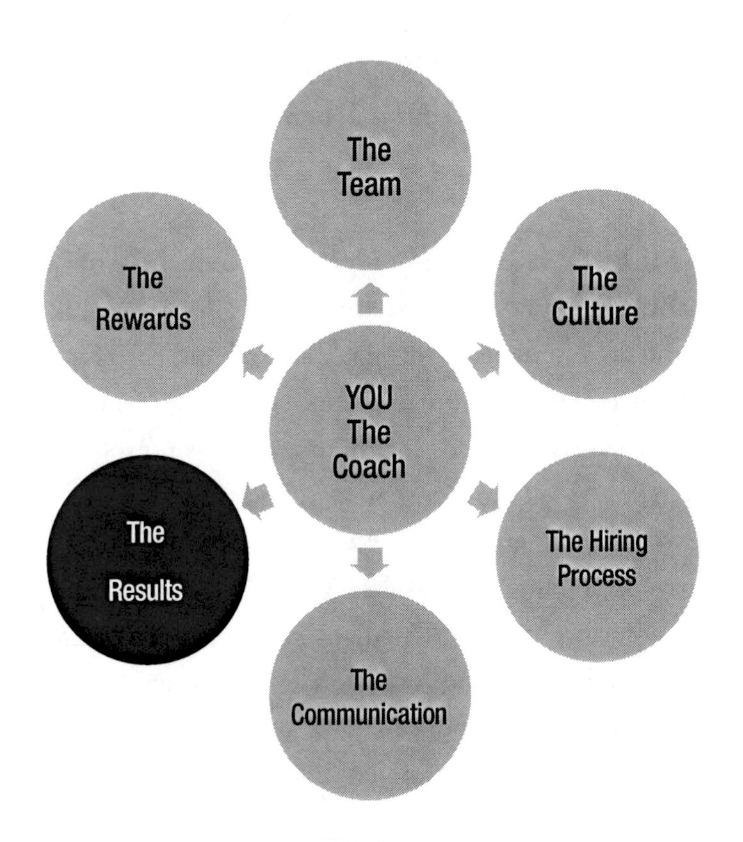

PUTTING NUMBERS ON THE BOARD

"Don't mistake activity for performance or busyness with results."

– John Wooden

NUMBERS ARE *EVERYTHING* in our line of work. Quantifiable results and activity directly affect everything we say and do. Numbers are the backbone of your career in sales, which makes the pressure to produce daunting at times. Even if you're consistently posting top numbers, you probably feel compelled to sell more and more... and more.

When is it enough? A few pep talks might stir up a frenzy of activity and results. Maybe what you need is a few more incentives. Or perhaps you aren't giving enough acknowledgement and accolades. A constant influx of encouragement, promotions, and other prizes might give your numbers the occasional boost, but none of those temporary motivators will deliver the long-term solutions you want and need.

Through a lot of trial and error, I realized that the answer to the question, "How can we put more numbers on the board?" didn't lie hidden within the next gimmick or motivational speech. I recognized that incentives, encouragement, and other external motivators are all part of the process, but they most certainly do not *define* that process—they merely play a supporting role in forming strong, consistently top-performing teams.

You need tangible sales management and training techniques in order to raise the bar on getting results and driving Top Performance.

I discovered some principles during my career that, once implemented, far surpassed the results gained by using any variety of external motivators. This chapter is all about the techniques and strategies I used over the years to produce successful, nationally recognized sales organizations year after year.

The Bedrock of Higher Numbers

Getting Elite results and staying at the top of the ranking reports isn't a simplistic 1-2-3 process. There are many pieces to the results puzzle and before you can even consider individual performance, you must make sure you have the basic groundwork of a high-performance team already in place. Here are the most important foundational keys to creating top results and producing the kinds of numbers that keep pipelines full and sales leaders and their teams happy:

Key #1: Employ an Exceptional Sales Manager

The reason that you, the sales leader, are at the heart of this book is because the foundation of Elite Sales Teams really does start with a great leader. Companies often promote their top salespeople into leadership positions. Although it could be argued that top salespeople make top leaders, I've seen this transition be wildly successful in some cases and wildly unsuccessful in others. Successful coaches are a lot more than just Top Performers with a new title. Not all sales people inherently have the coaching dexterity needed to effectively guide a team. So, if you are in a position to influence the hiring process for other managers and leaders, make sure you look for the right mix of talent, results, and other necessary qualities needed to make a great leader. For more on what it takes to be a great leader, refer to Secret One.

Key #2: Implement Individualized Management

If you want to improve results, one-size-fits-all incentive plans and group coaching will not always get you there. It's your job to deliver the same idea in a way that each team member can personally relate to. In other words: *Same message, different delivery.* Talk directly to the team to find out what makes their jobs challenging and how you can help them improve their performance. Work with each individual to learn how to effectively communicate with them, what drives them, and how they like and dislike being managed. Manage everyone individually, but with unbiased expectations and the same direct style of heartfelt communication. The strategies that work for one don't always work for another, so put a plan or strategy together to drive results for each team member. Once you hone in on their unique struggles or areas where they need more confidence, you can pair a struggling rep with the right Top Performers to give them the chance to see what it takes to over-achieve—and then coach them to take what they've learned and make it their own.

Key #3: Create the Right Team

Using a strong, systematic hiring process like the one outlined in Secret Four can help you hire the right people for your team every time. When you have communicated your expectations during the interview process, new hires know exactly what's in store for them. However, no matter how careful you are, there will be times when Low Performers exist on your on a team. Dealing with this will require a smarter approach than the one used by many other companies who spend so much time trying to coach Low Performers that they lose sight of the team as whole. Focus on who has the most potential and who is willing to do what it takes to succeed. Not everyone will. If they don't, you'll need to manage them out and replace the Low Performers with Top Performers. Not every Low Performer can be turned into a Top Performer through mentoring and coaching, but almost anyone who has the right mix of potential and drive can become a Top Performer with targeted coaching and improved focus.

Key #4: Consistent Focus on Activity

The right activity leads to the right results. If someone is struggling to get their numbers, there's a good chance they are either not doing the activity at all or they are doing the wrong activities. Review individual performance over the last thirty, sixty, ninety, 180, and 360 days. For each period, identify whether they show an increase, a decrease, or remain consistent for the most common sales activities (prospecting calls, appointments, closes, etc.). The key with monitoring these sales metrics is to make them a consistent part of the job—in the good times and the bad—so that they are viewed as a regular occurrence instead of a punishment. Always remind your team this is the first step to making money.

Key #5: Openly Disclose Performance

Make the team's performance known to all, either by group email or by posting results in the office. Knowing other people's activity and results gives reps a barometer for how they're doing compared to their peers. As a bonus, consistently posting daily or weekly performance can be an unspoken motivator. When everyone knows what everyone else is achieving in appointments and closing percentages, it can light a competitive fire. After all, who wants to see their name at the bottom of the list every week? It's healthy competition and it can give team members the small, subtle push they need to step up their performance.

Key #6: Do Pipeline Reviews

Consistently monitor and review pipelines. A hefty pipeline is the lifeline of any salesperson, so ask a lot of questions to identify what's real and what's fluff. Go through their pipelines together and get specific. Ask whom they've met with, how many times they've met, and if there were any reasons those clients would not want to buy from them. After doing this, I've discovered that some salespeople had much more in their pipeline than they realized, which can serve as a confidence booster and motivator. I've also learned that other pipelines were grossly inflated. Pipelines need to be robust and flowing. Always move accounts forward or up and out of the pipeline. If they aren't moving forward, ask your sales reps why and discuss what can be done to progress the account. Get to the bottom of the pipeline issue by asking questions: Why is the prospect not buying? What's really holding them back? What resources, if any, are needed to help close the opportunity?

Key #7: Get More Big Deals

Everyone on your team needs to search for the really big fabulous deals—BFD's. We're talking about those few large accounts that would make their quarter or their year. Once they get a taste of big deals, enormous successes, and the money and recognition that come with them, they'll want to find more. However, a word of caution here: If there is a lack of consistency in their performance, dig around to determine whether that stems from a weak pipeline or because they had a few large deals close without having smaller deals to fill in the gaps. If they have over achieved during a quarter due to a few large deals, find out if they would have still made their quota without those big deals. Relying on big deals alone is not a sustainable growth strategy, which is why it's critical to their success to have accounts and clients of all sizes.

Key #8: Do What Others Aren't

Can Friday's be fantastic? They sure can. It's all up to how you view them. As a general rule, salespeople tend to check out on Friday afternoons. But the last workday of the week was always a great closing day for my teams. While Low and Average Performers checked out on Fridays and pretended to work, my Top Performers were still hard at it. We set appointments and closed major deals right before the weekend. Why? Clients were in good moods because they were heading into the weekend and were looking to close the books on outstanding business. I love Fridays and with a little change in perspective, your team will also learn to love Fridays and see them for the fantastic, money making days they can be.

Key #9: Remove Obstacles

Fix problems, escalate and help resolve issues, help with and review pricing and proposals, do any and everything that removes roadblocks to winning the next deal. Do it in a timely manner. Be responsive.

Key #10: Develop Your Unique System

Every great sales leader needs their own set of processes that work like a well-oiled machine for the team. You and your team should know exactly how to do all aspects of your jobs, from the best ways to prospect to the steps for handling a customer complaint. Your system should also include installing a policy of exceptional customer service, accurate billing, how and when to use technology, where to go for help in every area of the business, and other support. All of these areas and more are imperative to a thriving sales organization. There is no wrong way to frame your unique system. What works for one team may not work for another. However, there are two things that will always work for anyone, any time, and anywhere—providing your team with every possible tool they need to succeed and taking the guesswork out of their daily duties and tasks. You've probably already put in the time, effort, sweat, and tears figuring out how to be fruitful in this business. Now you can help pave the way for the next generation of Top Performers on your team by setting them up to succeed with elements of the unique system that worked for you.

How you position the ten keys above is critical. If you use performance-enhancing tactics in order to micromanage or remind team members of their lack of performance, they won't want to discuss their results or participate and they'll view the entire process as a punishment. But if you approach these strategies as a way to work together to produce top results, they will become highly effective tools for propelling performance.

PROPELLING PERFORMANCE

Secret Performance Killers

Throughout my career, I found that each of the ten keys to top performance were essential to my team's success. I also discovered some sales tactics that consistently detracted from performance and had to be removed.

Don't use fancy tricks.
Go back to the basics.

If you have a team of *potential* Top Performers that need to become a group of *actual* Top Performers, you must dig deeper to see what is holding them back. Here are a few of the most notorious offenders when it comes to stifling performance and hindering success to be mindful of:

- **Fancy Selling.** A lot of leaders and teams default to

"getting fancy" when numbers start to fall. People think that if they come up with fifty new ways to sell or memorize thirty new closes, sales will skyrocket. You may achieve some success from these maneuvers, but I've never had any luck with gimmicks. That's the problem with gimmicks—you are relying on *luck*, not skill. Clients know when they're being bamboozled. Learn how to professionally prospect, set appointments, foster relationships, deliver a great pitch, and close. That approach may not be fancy, but it works.

- **Desperate Selling.** Just as leadership often defaults to micromanaging when numbers start to decline, salespeople frequently default to desperation selling when they aren't meeting quotas. You can hear it in their voices—and so can clients. Desperate salespeople also have the tendency to over-share during a sale. They'll tell a prospect how they get paid or inform clients they would be helping them make their quota by saying, "Yes." Our job is to offer value and service to clients. Winning teams know how to discover what's in it for the client. Let your team know they will be better off acting as if they are already overachieving and don't need the sale rather than resort to desperation tactics. Where do they get that level of confidence when they're underperforming? They get it from you. When times are tough, give more encouragement and more support, not less. Remind salespeople they can do it. Then show them *how* they can do it. They won't act desperate when they no longer *feel* desperate.

- **Complicated Selling.** One of the fastest ways to lose clients and solid team members is to make things overly complicated. Salespeople who master the art of keeping their pitch and presentation simple will close more and close faster. Those who complicate the process can talk clients right out of the deal. Keep it simple.
- **Attachment Selling.** Attachment selling is similar to desperate selling. Salespeople can get so attached to a deal that they find it difficult to move on. They must learn how to recognize when a sale is over, when it's appropriate to continue nurturing the opportunity, and when it's the right time to walk away. Help your team recognize when to move on. If they have enough opportunities in their pipeline, they won't need to hold on so tightly to each opportunity. Help them see there are more fish in the sea. My motto is "cut bait." Know when to 'cut bait' without losing momentum and help your team move on to other viable opportunities. The best way to do this is to move right on to the next opportunity. Momentum is the cure for many an ailment in the world of professional selling.

- **Price Tag Selling.** Even if you're selling a commodity or a product that is price sensitive, your team must be experts at building the value over being price focused. Price tag selling is like flipping over your Royal Flush for all to see and then placing your bet instead of keeping a poker face and going all-in to win. Be sure that your team isn't showing their hand too early in the presentation. If they are, they stand to lose the entire deal. If they build enough value before they talk price, salespeople increase their odds of closing. Value can outsell price.
- **Micromanagement.** Being a micromanager is one of the most surefire ways to stifle performance. The trademark symptoms of micromanagement are a general lack of help and guidance, the absence of support, low team energy levels, and limited engagement from the leader. No one likes to be micromanaged (including you), so ensure you retire this technique for good.
- **Lack of Preparation.** It just doesn't pay to wing it. When you walk into a sales meeting or presentation unprepared, you're lucky if the deal turns into a win. More often than not, being unprepared results in the loss of a sale, as well as a good prospect and possible source of referrals. I've been on appointments where clients wanted to buy, but the reps didn't have the proper paperwork to close the deal. Their lack of

preparation caused both them and the client to walk away unsatisfied. Not good.

- **Biased Quotas.** Just as territory assignments must be fair, so too must quotas. A swift way to tank results is to provide biased quotas based on where salespeople fall in the rankings. One of my former companies assigned higher quotas to their Top Performers, which seemed grossly unfair and was certainly a demotivator for the overachievers. They also provided low or no increases to the quotas of Low Performers. Quotas should be fair, unbiased, and based on a transparent system that is easy to understand.

These productivity killers are common companions of sales teams across the country. The only way to make sure they don't manifest themselves on your team is to not engage in any of these activities yourself. When you do that, you can coach your team on how to steer clear of them as well.

Serious Performance Boosters

Top Performance starts with high levels of activity. Of course, that means that Top Managers must carefully monitor the activity of each person on their team. Managing activity can be a joy or sorrow. If this is an area where you would like to improve, here is a new perspective on managing activity that might help:

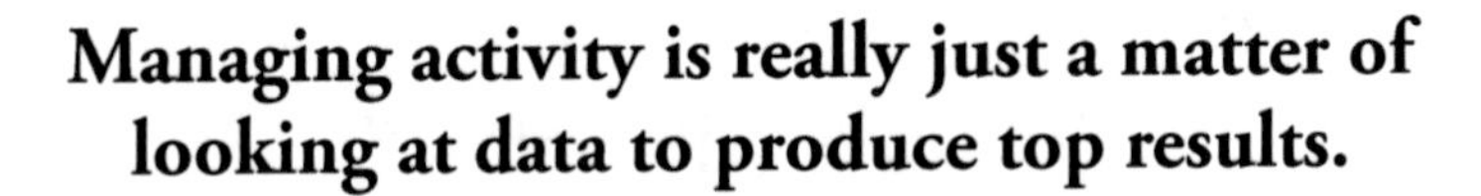

Managing activity is really just a matter of looking at data to produce top results.

It's not a popularity contest. It's objective and factual. You're checking to see if individuals did or didn't meet a specific target. Better activity leads to sales. By looking at the numbers, you can determine if success is on the horizon. Below are the areas I focus on to effectively manage activity and boost results:

- **Ample Appointments.** This is a straightforward performance boosting technique: Set more appointments. If your team isn't going on enough appointments, it will be tough to stay at the top of the rankings. Teach them to look for *quantity* first, and then explain that *quality* will come after they make appointment-setting a natural and consistent part of their business. Every person on your team should have a goal set for appointments each day or week based on the typical appointment-to-sale ratio in your company or industry.
- **Balanced Territories.** Territory issues can be complex, but the key is to ensure that each person has the properly sized territory or account base to achieve his or her quota. If not, make the proper adjustments so that territories are fair and equitable

across the board. I have seen several high quality performers lose jobs due to lack of performance. It wasn't the rep. It was their account base or territory. Ensure territories and quotas are as equitable as possible so all reps are set up to succeed.

- **Big Deals.** Does each of your salespeople have one or more big deals in his or her pipeline that are realistic and attainable? To ensure they do, help your team members develop a Top 10 Target List of BFD's (Big Fabulous Deals) to focus on. It will help them stay motivated by keeping the large strategic sales at the top of their list of priorities. Depending on your product or service and the length of your sales cycle, it could be a list you plan to close each month, quarter, or year. A Top Ten Target List should be a requirement for all sales reps. It will help them manage their time and their pipeline by getting them laser-focused on the ten specific accounts they will target to close within a specific time period.
- **Positive Working Environment.** Your working environment plays a very important role in your success. Your reps will thrive when they work in an environment that pushes them, challenges them, holds them accountable, and keeps them on their toes. It is also beneficial to be surrounded by people and leadership that they like and respect—people who make them feel empowered, heard, and important.

- **A Leader Who is a Partner.** The term "boss" has a negative connotation. It denotes authority and power over other people. As the leader of your sales team, you are not their boss; you are a business partner who helps them achieve their goals and provides coaching, support, and encouragement when needed.
- **Helpful Reviews.** Does your company complete formal annual or semi-annual performance reviews? The purpose of such reviews is to help employees learn their strengths and their areas of opportunity. Of course, reviews aren't always seen as a positive, since they really only boost morale when a rep receives a glowing review. One way to make sure that reviews are helpful rather than harmful is to schedule them regularly. Performance reviews are a time to give feedback about specific areas of that need improvement as well as a time to praise reps for things they are doing right and for their contributions. You can quickly review your current performance reviews and their effectiveness by asking yourself questions like:
    - Do I only give performance reviews when performance is trailing off, or do I give them regularly, no matter what?
    - How often do I provide performance reviews? Is it enough? Too much?
    - What criteria (numbers, production,

quotas, pipeline, etc.) do I use to provide feedback? Do I use the same criteria to review every single rep?

- Do people leave performance reviews clear on what they need to do to become Top Performers?

- **Frequent Recognition**. It's vital you have a consistent and effective recognition program. Start by finding out how each individual likes to be recognized. Some people love it; others really don't feel comfortable with a lot of recognition, especially in a public setting. Either way, it's still necessary for every rep to receive some form of acknowledgement. Never forget to recognize support staff and other internal staff that help you close business as well. Throughout my career, I created a variety of recognition categories to give everyone a chance to receive accolades, not just Top Performers. The final Secret in this book will cover recognition and rewards in more detail. The most important thing to remember is to shower people with thanks. The possibilities for what you have to thank them for are endless—thank them for their efforts, for trying something new, for accomplishing a personal goal, and for both small and large achievements.

NETWORKING = MORE LEADS AND REFERRALS

The race to meet quotas, call on new prospects, service existing clients, and stay at the top of the rankings is never ending. We all know there's limited time to accomplish all the things we need to get done on a daily basis, which is why we often need the help of those around us. It's also one of the main reasons why we work in teams. Having other people's backs and helping others succeed aren't merely selfless acts—they benefit *everyone* involved. It's a breath of fresh air for salespeople to know they can count on others. You can promote this type of structure within your organization by sharing beneficial information, providing leads, and exchanging help—otherwise known as networking.

When it comes to networks, reciprocity is the name of the game. Networking is more successful when you convey the fact that you are doing it to help others and not just to get more leads, referrals, or assistance for yourself.

A Web of Internal Networks

Successful networking starts within your company. Who can help you find leads? Who can help you close business? Who needs to be involved in the sale to assist with technology, proposals, pricing, and approvals? Those are the people who should be part of your core internal networking group.

Building and nurturing your internal network list is vital to achieving Top Performance. An *Internal Network* is a group of people in your company with whom you communicate on a regular basis and who help you do your job better. Depending upon the size of your company, the individuals who form your internal communication network could be IT, technology support, subject matter experts, marketing, human resources, operations, sales support, administrative support, peers within and outside your geographic territory, Top Performers and leaders in the same or other markets, customer service, and others.

Begin building your internal networking group by creating an organizational "Who To Call" chart for support in the areas of customer service, technology, and the other areas listed in the previous paragraph. When you complete this list, distribute it to your entire sales organization so that everyone knows exactly who to call when they need help, support, or guidance.

A Web of External Networks

External networking will help you find a variety of like-minded people willing to work together and exchange leads. Some of the largest deals my teams ever closed were leads from what I call "strategic partners," people who sell and service accounts you also target and sell to (and to the same decision makers). Here are some ways to begin recognizing and growing your external network of strategic partners:

- Strategic partners can be those calling on the same decision makers and clients as you are and those who align with your account base or territory.

- Find them by looking at sign-in sheets to see who signed in before you when you go to appointments with prospects and clients. If someone just met with the same person you are there to see, find out what business he or she is in and how you can help each other exchange leads.
- Directly ask clients who their other reps are. If you did a good job of building the relationship, they'll gladly give you helpful contact information or a lead from time to time.

Why would people want to partner with you and provide you with insights and leads? It's simple: They will help you because you will help them. It's a reciprocal relationship. Others do it because of an incentive offer. Some are offered gifts, money, gift cards, or other incentives for providing qualified leads that close. Communicate with others from the beginning of the partnership that your intention is to help each other, and you will find networking to be a fulfilling and lucrative business practice

Building Connections

The key to growing both internal and external networks is a concept called Duplication of Effort. When certain activity gets results, you want more of it, and you want it consistently. That's where networking can play a vital role in your business. Elite Performers find, grow, and successfully maintain open communication with people in their networks to increase their spheres of influence, exchange leads, expand their business, and duplicate their efforts.

Elite Performers master their duplication of effort.

Sales may be cutthroat, but most people derive satisfaction from helping others. In fact, most of us have probably witnessed that the best way to *get* help from others is by *giving* it with no expectations. For example, make a phone call to check in on a client for no other reason than to say hello and ask whether you can help in some way. This serves a dual purpose: It reestablishes communication with an existing client and displays the fact that you are there to serve others.

Small steps that foster open communication and mutual reciprocity go a long way toward promoting the kind of networking that grows and maintains a healthy pipeline of leads and a full calendar of lucrative activity. I've seen that taking the time to build these valuable relationships can pay off. To get more, you must give more:

- Make a conscious effort to have your meet with your networking partners in person when possible, or call them.
- Ensure your team is consistent, not haphazard with

their efforts. Schedule networking calls and meetings so that they are a regular part of their workweek.

- As a leader, you'll most likely need to lead the networking initiative on your team. Connect with peers who align with your team, and show the salespeople on your team how to get the most out of networking through leading by example.
- Take the extra steps to coordinate mixers, networking lunches, happy hours, or dinners.

Networking is two-way communication, not a one-way street.

Networking is only as powerful as you and your reps make it. Reps have come to me in the past to say they've "tried networking" but were disappointed because they didn't get any leads. I asked how many leads they gave out and how often they connected, only to find out they gave few to none and met only once or twice a year. As a leader, those are the type of questions you want to consistently ask. You also want to quantify the following:

- The number of partners they're teaming with
- The number of leads given versus the number of leads received

- The number of times they met with or called each partner

When done properly, quality networking can pay off in a big way and it can help you and your team drive top results.

A Web of Referrals

Referrals are the lifeblood of any sales organization. Prospecting is important, but the ability to gather referrals is what separates the ranking risers from the rest of the pack. Existing clients are the most obvious referral source, but you and your team can also get them from lots of other sources including prospects that don't say "Yes."

Here is how you can help your team communicate in a way that gets more referrals in order to keep their pipelines robust and healthy:

- **Keep in Touch.** Send email updates to existing clients on a consistent basis to keep you and your company fresh in their minds. That way when you do regularly ask for referrals, the response won't be, "Now, remind me who you are again?"
- **Just Ask.** It's such a simple, but all too often skipped step. Never leave a successful client meeting without asking for more referrals. Satisfied clients will be happy to help you.
- **Show Them Lists.** Take printed lists of your Top 10 targeted clients and show the names to other clients

and prospects to see if they know anyone on the list who can help with an introduction.

- **Use Social Media.** Use LinkedIn and other social media to reach out to your prospects and clients depending on your industry and company size.

When done properly and consistently, asking for referrals can also pay off in a big way and it can help you and your team drive top results.

A Web of Events

Although networking events should never be your teams sole means of networking, they are an important aspect of your networking and prospecting efforts. In fact, although you may not walk in and automatically find a room full of qualified prospects waiting to sign a proposal, events are some of the best places to open up the lines of communication with potential strategic partners and find new referral sources and clients. You can even host your own events that encourage partnering, collaborating, and information sharing.

Networking events also help your team stay social and can ensure that they keep their communication skills sharp. Salespeople often work virtually behind their phones and laptops, and they use Skype, webinars, and teleseminars to communicate and connect. Sometimes all of today's technology can detach your team from actively seeking human-to-human communication. They can't hide behind their laptop when they are in a room full of potential clients and partners.

TURNING LOW PERFORMERS INTO TOP PERFORMERS

The way to stay on the top of the ranking report is to have everyone on your team contribute 100%. Of course, that's an ideal scenario. We know there is no such thing as the perfect team that will stay with you for the duration of your career. Low Performance happens, even to the most Elite of the Elite. So, it's time to determine which category each person on your team fits into, where their deficits are, and what direction, if any, you need to move them.

You may sense that some of your Average and Low Performers really want to be part of the team and have the desire to succeed. In such cases, you have to decide how to move them up the ranking reports. Your Top Performers may need to keep doing exactly what they are doing with occasional help and coaching from you. Or it may be time to move them over to other positions and possibly to a leadership role if they are qualified. For some of your Low Performers, it may be time to actually move them out and on to a career that benefits them and your team.

When salespeople are not performing well they are fully aware of it. Their paychecks as well as their lack of motivation, momentum, and confidence serve as reminders. A Low Performer already knows he or she is a Low Performer and doesn't need any additional reminders from you. The old way of handling Low Performance was to micromanage. A more effective way is to encourage, support, and work together.

Above all, let Low Performers know you're there to help and serve them. People ask me all the time how to create a Top Performer out of a Low Performer. When working with Low or Average Performers who truly desire to improve, I have developed a ten-part process that is highly effective:

1. **Go Back to Basics.** When in doubt, go back to the basics. Re-examine and reset results in the least complicated and most fundamental way—by starting with proper sales training and a results-based approach. The basics of selling really boil down to an understanding that their career is a numbers game. Without the right activity and the right numbers, success in selling is highly unlikely. Ensure they talk to other Top Performers for help and advice. Ask them to share with you what they learned from these conversations. Encourage them to read motivational and success books to remind them of the fundamental attitudes and perspectives that shape Top Performers.
2. **Identify The Gaps in Activity.** More activity always produces more sales. Make sure Low Performers are making a sufficient amount of prospecting calls, meeting with the proper decision makers, sending emails, canvassing their territory, getting referrals, working with partners, networking, and requesting appointments. They need to do this consistently, because inconsistent activity can quickly lead to low

performance.

3. **Help Improve Their Pitch.** How is their presentation? A good pitch is fundamental to all sales success. Low Performers are often in need of refining their pitch, so attend appointments with them and work with them individually to see where problems exist. For more on the pitch, see Secret Two.
4. **Help Them With Their Close**. If a Low Performer is setting a sufficient number of appointments but closing very few, the issue likely rests with the close. Examine their closing percentages, help them learn how to close at the right time, and make sure they are actually asking for the sale.
5. **Simplify the Sales Process**. It's possible that Low Performers are complicating the sales process so much that prospects are saying "No" or "Not Now" simply because they are confused or overwhelmed. Ensure that Low Performers know how to identify and eliminate the performance stifling sales strategies and fancy selling tactics mentioned in the previous sections.
6. **Analyze their Progress.** Regularly monitor Low Performers progress based on their numbers and facts, not on if you personally like them or not. Monitor their activity weekly by using the techniques, evaluation and sales guidelines presented

in Secret Two. Be sure to review their pipeline and determine whether it is robust enough to hit targets. Closely monitor and discuss all opportunities in their 30/60/90/180 day pipelines. Is their performance trending upward, downward, or remaining flat? The answer to that question will allow you to determine how to best spend your coaching time with them.

7. **Overcoming Objections**. It's vital your team become experts at overcoming the most common objections from prospects. They must be excellent at this to win. This is one area where I've witnessed Low Performers struggle. They can't find the right words or positioning to overcome prospects objections. Top Performers can easily respond. They expect objections they'll get and practice how to respond.

8. **Encourage Open Communication.** Ask what Low Performers would like help with versus telling them what areas need they need to work on. Question them as to how you can help or who else might be able to. If they don't answer, nudge them. Ask if there's something currently getting in the way of their success. By doing this I was often able to find out when personal issues were impacting someone's ability to focus on the job. Getting difficult personal issues out in the open often helps reps stop dwelling on them and refocus on the task at hand. You're not trying to pry into people's personal lives. You're

asking because you want to see them succeed. If they flourish, so do you.

9. **Create Top Ten Lists.** Work with each salesperson to create a Top Ten list of ideal customers for them to focus on so they can maximize results. Have struggling team members concentrate on closing one large deal at a time. Don't overwhelm them by making goals too high. Keep them realistic and achievable. Then track and discuss weekly whether or not they achieved these goals. If they are still unable to reach any of the big prospects on their Top Ten List after several weeks or months, step in and contact the prospect yourself. Ask partners if they can help with a warm introduction. You can also go back to one of the previous steps to figure out where things are going awry.

10. **Get Help.** Even when you are the leader, you don't have to go it alone. In some cases, it's okay to call for backup and bring in peers and other leaders to help train and mentor Low Performers. No leader is an island. In fact, the best leaders have mentors and coaches in place at all times to help with tough decisions and provide answers when their own solutions seem to be missing the mark. No one person has all the answers and your team doesn't expect perfection—so get help when you need it. As leaders, we're often so focused on helping

everyone else. It's nice to have someone there to help us when we need it.

You can follow these steps in an informal setting, in the field, and during strategy or one-on-one sessions where you can discuss roadblocks, challenges, and the resources and steps required to boost results.

And remember: Your reps are more likely to listen to you when you present yourself as a partner, not a micromanaging boss. Emphasize that you are a team and teams work together to succeed. Avoid giving off the "you work *for* me" vibe and remind them you are there to help *them* reach *their* goals, not yours. Work together to show that you care about them as a person more than you care about their results.

Knowing When It's Time to Let Go

Despite your best efforts to help, there will be times when you need to let people go. You may find that you have someone on your team who is a great fit within your company, just not in their current position. In such cases, the best thing to do is allow them to thrive in a different position within your organization. If you come to the conclusion that a team member simply isn't a fit at all, do what's best for both them and your organization and encourage them to look for a position elsewhere where they may be more successful.

Whatever the reason you have for moving someone over or out, start the process at the first possible opportunity. Depending on your company's HR policies, it could take anywhere from thirty to 120 days before you can officially put them through the proper HR termination or relocation process. That could already be more time than you or the rep is willing to wait, which is just one reason why you must move swiftly. Here are several other reasons why it's best to act quickly:

- To be fair to the employee and allow that person to thrive in another position within the same company or somewhere else
- To be fair to the others on the team who *are* producing
- To do what's best for the team, clients, and future prospects
- To help the profits and revenues of the company

Not every relationship works out. Just because someone is a Low Performer on your team doesn't mean they are a Low Performer in any other role in their lives. It's part of an Elite Leader's job description to be honest, caring, and understanding when having candid conversations with Low Performers. Their true calling may be waiting for them at their next job, which means that sometimes you have to let them go in order to succeed elsewhere. If they want to leave, wish them the absolute best. But if they want to stay:

Be crystal clear that all levels of performers must give 100% each day they are on your team.

You may have already faced a situation where a Low Performer was putting in the time and even doing the right activity, but their attitude and intangible qualities weren't the right fit for the job. Just as couples regularly separate due to irreconcilable differences, it happens in business as well. Forcing the wrong relationship to function will never work. Some people don't get along and never will. In such cases, it's best they move on and find a healthy relationship that *will* be successful. Here are some prime examples of when you need to move them out:

- They are unwilling to be coached.
- They will not listen to feedback or guidance.
- They are not open to any kind of change.
- They are simply not willing to do the work.
- They display a perpetually negative attitude.
- They blame others for failures instead of taking personal responsibility.
- They have ongoing personality conflicts with you, other team members, internal staff,

prospects or clients.

- They are someone who may be a close friend but who is not producing.

In many cases, it is easy to let your personal affinities stand in the way of making the best decision for you, for the Low Performers, and for the team. Those serious talks can become excruciating if you have to discipline or fire a dear friend, so try not to get too close to your direct reports.

Document important conversations, especially when people are on their way out. It's wise to know company policies and procedures for managing performance and behaviors. Be aware of the things you can do or say that could land you in what I affectionately call "HR Jail." My system for tracking conversations is simple: Create a document for each rep and save it with their name as the file name. Prior to each conversation, open the document and type what was discussed directly in the document during each meeting or conversation. If you ever need to go to HR, all pertinent information will be in one document. This will save you countless hours of digging for details and facts.

You can have a positive and immediate affect on your team's results and their numbers by incorporating even a few of these strategies I developed over many years. Your team has talent and potential that is waiting to be tapped and you can help them achieve as much success as they desire.

IT'S YOUR TURN

There is no issue too big or too small to bring up when it comes to driving results—because results are what drive the bottom line. Here is some additional food for thought and some questions to get you thinking about results:

How do you currently evaluate your employees' results? How well does that approach work in determining how to boost those results?

____

____

____

How often do you provide feedback to each of your team members based on their numbers? Is it in a formal or informal setting or performance review? Should you be doing that more or less often? Are you doing it too often or not enough?

____

____

____

Do you post performance and results for everyone on the team to see? If so, what do you notice about the team's reactions to those postings? Do you think it's helpful for them to see everyone else's numbers?

____

____

____

How much time do you currently spend with your reps discussing their pipelines? Is it the right amount, too much, or not enough?

____

____

____

Does your team using selling techniques that kill performance? How can you coach your team to avoid them?

____

____

____

What performance-boosting strategy has worked well for you in the past? How can you utilize that approach more fully in the future?

____

____

____

How do you handle low performing team members? What additional steps can you take to help them improve their performance?

____

____

____

When you recognize that it's time to move them out, how quickly do you act and what steps do you take? How can you improve that process in the future?

____

____

____

SECRET 7

IT'S ALL ABOUT THE REWARDS

THE BEST PART OF THE JOB

"People work for money, but go the extra mile for recognition, praise, and rewards."
—Dale Carnegie

AS A SALES leader, you play a key role in influencing the performance of your salespeople. We've talked about numerous ways you can drive top performance in the previous chapters. Now we come to the one I think is the most important, the most powerful, and the most fun—rewarding and recognizing your people for their efforts.

Rewards and recognition are essential to creating an Elite Sales Team.

Salespeople want to feel that their contributions are valued. Everyone has the need to be acknowledged and to feel a sense of achievement for a job well done or even for a courageous effort. People who don't feel valued rarely make a significant difference. But those who do feel appreciated will always do more than what's expected. In this way, an effective employee reward and recognition plan can significantly improve work performance and motivate team members. This is why a reward and recognition plan should be an integral component of your management strategy.

The key to creating an effective reward and recognition plan lies in understanding what drives salespeople to excel. Compensation certainly plays a crucial role in propelling performance, but it's only one piece of the puzzle. Awards, praise, and a positive work environment are also important for encouraging salespeople to always give their best effort.

In this chapter, we'll explore all of these aspects of creating reward and recognition plans, why they're important, and how you can put them to work for you to inspire Low and Average Performers to become Top Performers and ensure Top Performers stay that way. Let's start with compensation.

SHOW THEM THE MONEY

It's time to talk about the best part of sales, the part that most people just can't get enough of. I'm talking, of course, about compensation. Your team works hard for their paychecks—

because capital, currency, cash, or whatever name you call it is the means for securing the rewards we all want in life. Top Performers want the freedom, fun, and recognition that all come from increasing their bottom line.

In all my years in sales, I've found that salespeople are in it, first and foremost, for the money. In fact, research indicates that money is the number one motivator of salespeople.[4] Reps are willing to learn from the best, stay coachable, and to listen to what you have to say in order to increase the size of their paychecks. Unfortunately, most sales leaders have little say in creating the compensation plans for their people. So rewarding your salespeople with raises, bonuses, and other monetary incentives are most likely off the table. But that doesn't mean there's nothing you can do.

You can reward your team members by showing them how to earn the highest commissions. Elite Leaders are intimately familiar with their reps' compensation plan. They know what pays the most money and that's what they coach their people to sell. If you want to drive top performance, align your coaching and mentoring with the products and services that pay the highest commissions. This not only rewards your team members by putting more money in their pockets, it also lets them know that you have their best interests at heart.

---

4 Peter Ostrow, "Motivate, Incent, Compensate, Enable: Sales Performance Management Best Practices" (Aberdeen Group, 2013), 12.

SHOW THEM SOME LOVE

Money may be the ultimate motivator—but running a close second is recognition. We all want to be recognized, thanked, and appreciated for our work, and dedication. When we aren't, we tend to ask ourselves, "Why am I doing this? Nobody cares." On the other hand, a Gallup poll found that 82% of employees say that recognition or praise they receive at work motivates them to improve their performance.

That's why you shouldn't let a day or week pass without recognizing everyone around you for the work they do, the support they give, and the results they achieve. This includes your team, sales support, technical staff, peers, leaders, and the various departments in your organization including marketing, operations, customer service, and all the others who helped you along the way.

Recognition doesn't have to be elaborate; it just needs to happen. It can be as simple as copying upper management on an email to let them know that a specific rep was a key player in a sale. Straightforward things like this go a long way. When people receive recognition, it makes them want to do more for you over someone who doesn't appear to appreciate their efforts. During my career as a Top Performer, I rarely had anyone thank me or recognize me for my performance and results. So, I've always tried to remain extremely conscious of the amount of recognition I give out, even for the small things and for minor progress. I never want my people to feel the sting of not being recognized for a job well done, so I strive to be a "thanks machine" whenever I can.

I worked for someone for three years, and yet I knew nothing more than the general area of town in which he lived and that the he was married with a few children. Anytime we met, there was *zero* chitchat or small talk. There were no polite questions like, "How was your weekend?" It was all business, all the time—and it wasn't fun. The relationship felt incredibly impersonal. It also made it hard to take any thanks or gratitude from this manager—which were few and far between—with any sincerity. I didn't need to know my boss's shoe size, what was on his DVR, or the play-by-play of his weekend agenda. I just wanted to feel he was human and that he saw me as a human being as well. I wanted to be a person, not just an employee. I wanted to have at least some kind of personal connection but there was none.

It wouldn't have taken much for us to get to know each other better, but he didn't even take five minutes out of his day to show an interest in me as a person. Just remember this: Learn enough about your rep's lives so that your recognition can come from a sincere place of caring about them as an individual.

Creating a Formal Recognition Plan

Recognition is not a "nice to have." It's a key reward that your team is working to receive. Ensure you have a formal recognition program in place that promotes recognition at every level and in every form—written, verbal, and in-person, whether your company promotes this or not. I know there are times when getting recognized in front of a group is embarrassing. I've never been great at receiving public praise—but I'm working on it. Your reps may feel the same way. So take the time to find out what works for each individual.

Even though there's only one #1 spot, every person on your team deserves *some* kind of recognition. Performance is one area to formally recognize, but it is not the only thing that should be praised. You also need to recognize Low and Average Performers, not just Top Performers, for their victories because every team member's actions contribute to the success of the team. If salespeople don't feel recognized for their hard work and effort, it doesn't motivate them to push hard to excel and climb to the top. They'll simply think, "I can never beat that guy or gal, so why should I even try?" When you praise team members for even the smallest accomplishments or improvements, they will try even harder because once someone gets a taste of recognition; they'll want more and put in the work to get it. That's why it's so important to reward effort as well as successes.

**Celebrate the small accomplishments.
All those small accomplishments
add up to big accomplishments.**

If you find yourself always patting the back of one or two team members for their big accomplishments, you may be giving the impression that you play favorites. This will do you no favors in terms of building trust and team cohesion. Your Top Performers deserve recognition because they earn it with their performance, but it's important to give recognition to everyone regardless of tenure, performance, or the size of the achievement.

When I lead a group, there is no accomplishment too small for some recognition. The limelight can and must be shared, so I use a variety of ways to deliver appreciation, and I do so publically and privately, as well as verbally and in writing. Here are some great ways to show your team how much you appreciate their efforts, not just their results:

- **Praise them to upper management.** Send an email praising a rep's success or progress, and copy your leader. You can also copy leaders above your leader and leaders of everyone who played a role in helping a large deal close.
- **Hand out certificates and trophies.** Sales reps enjoy tangible representations of their achievements. A certificate or trophy they can display in their office is an excellent way to recognize and reward their efforts. Every time they see it, they'll be reminded of how receiving recognition felt and want more. It can also encourage others who want similar recognition to work harder. You can have

certificates printed professionally or you can create free certificates online. If you have the budget, give engraved trophies. They'll have the greatest impact. If you need to keep an eye on costs, you can have one trophy that revolves to different reps each week, month or quarter, based on how often you recognize your team.

- **Send a handwritten note.** Never underestimate the power of getting a handwritten note in the mail. It could be better than a birthday card to team members who are working hard.
- **Flex a little on hours.** If there's one reward that rises above the rest, it's flexible work schedules. Flextime is a perk that offers the most gain with the least pain. If your company allows it, give a little latitude in determining work schedules and when team members can take time for family or personal issues. As long as the employee doesn't abuse the privilege, this can go a long way to building trust and prove how much you value their efforts. It's likely your employee is working extra hours throughout the week as it is. Just make sure whatever you do falls in line with HR and company policies.
- **Blow out the candles.** Make sure you recognize every employee's birthday and work anniversary in some way. It goes a long way toward making someone feel special.

- **Applaud their efforts—literally.** If someone has done something really worthwhile, have your entire staff give him or her a standing ovation at the next meeting. (But first make sure they are comfortable receiving public recognition. If they aren't, this may start getting them used to it.)
- **Elect them to the Wall of Fame.** Set aside a public space inside your workplace and hang photos of employees who've accomplished something truly special, along with the details of what they did to earn their place on the wall. If you're in a virtual environment, send out monthly "Wall of Fame" recognition emails that serve a similar purpose. Either way make sure to reward more than just rankings. You can recognize individuals for providing stellar customer service, retaining a client who threatened to leave, helping another team member close a big sale, or for going above and beyond the call of duty. That way every team member, not just Top Performers, can have a chance to find a place of honor on the wall.
- **Publicize their successes.** Publicly recognize employees so the whole company, department, region, and team can share in their accomplishments. Put their efforts (not just results) in an email or monthly newsletter.
- **Remember the secret words.** The two most

underused words in the corporate world that get the highest return on investment and return on your time are the simple words "thank you." You can never say it enough.

- **Invite them to a meeting.** Allow a team member to participate in a leader meeting with your peers. It will not only give them insight into what happens on those calls and meetings, it will also give them exposure to other managers and executives.

These are just a few examples of how you can reward and recognize your reps. With a little imagination, you can probably come up with plenty more.

A "thank you" or a figurative or literal pat on the back goes a long way toward motivating your team. In fact, recognition is second only to compensation when it comes to motivation. When you shower your team with sincere recognition of their efforts and accomplishments, it lights a fire inside that keeps them going to earn even greater recognition down the road.

CREATE A POSITIVE WORKING ENVIRONMENT

Money and recognition are excellent ways to both reward and drive Top Performance. But, there is another, less tangible, yet highly effective way you can reward your team members and inspire them to excel. Create a positive environment that makes it easier for them to do their jobs and helps them feel good about getting up and coming to work in the morning. Here are few techniques and strategies you can use that will help create a positive work environment that will propel your team to greater performance.

Be a Good Listener

If your team members think they are not being heard, it makes them feel they aren't being valued which can lead to unhappiness and dissatisfaction in the workplace, neither of which are good for driving top performance. The best way to ensure your people know that you value their concerns, emotions, and feelings, is to take the time to stop and listen, really listen, to what they have to say. That means making good eye contact, escaping the lure of multi-tasking, avoiding checking your phone during the conversation, and offering a reply that is based directly on what someone has just shared with you, rather than giving a canned response.

Always Get Both Sides of the Story

Whether something happens internally within your team or company or externally with a client, getting both sides of the story is imperative to creating a positive work environment. Jumping to conclusions never leads to the best outcome. In fact, it can cause irreparable damage to relationships. No one likes to be falsely accused and you can lose credibility and trust if you don't ask to hear both sides of a dispute.

Let's say a client calls to complain about an issue (and it

could be a legitimate problem), but as they complain, they throw you or someone on your team under the bus to get what they want. They know the mantra, "The customer is always right," and they think they'll get their way if they press hard enough. Well, even though the customer is our first priority in sales, customers and clients are not *always* right at the expense of everyone else. You can make concessions as long as they don't require sacrificing someone else's good name and reputation. There are always two sides to every story, so make it a consistent habit to let everyone involved tell their version of the truth before being quick to make a potentially inaccurate conclusion.

Encourage Hard Work and More Play

Many of us get caught in the swamp of overworking to succeed and to earn those coveted and sought-after rewards. However, working 24/7 isn't good for any profession. When doctors and nurses are overworked, their judgment and precision suffers. When you work 24/7, you run the risk of missing out on some of the greatest rewards and you can put your career and your team's Elite status at risk. If your team sees you firing off emails during nights and weekends, they'll think that they must do the same—and to me, that is just not healthy. It will cause burnout, lack of enthusiasm, and overall demotivation.

You can still earn the rewards you desire without working around the clock.

Work-life balance is more vital today than ever before in a society that promotes a non-stop pace. We discussed the concept of workaholism and its pitfalls in Secret One. It's something I have to be conscious of almost every day because I tend to gravitate toward workaholism. If you can relate, you know how easy it is to get sucked into working too much.

According to the U.S. Travel Association, approximately ninety-six percent of American workers say they recognize the need for taking time off (and actually do see it as a reward for a job well done). Yet more than forty-one percent of those workers let their PAID vacation days go unused every year.[5] This is tragic and must change. Those paid days off are one of the reasons you and your team are working so hard. So, tell your people to stop working when it's been too long since their last break from the grind. Encourage them to manage their PTO throughout the year, go on vacation, and take off the time from work they've earned so they can come back refueled, reenergized, and motivated.

The younger generation, also known as Millennials (born between 1980-2000), entering the workforce seems to know

5 "Overwhelmed America: Why Don't We Use Our Earned Leave?" *Project: Time Off.* Presented by GfK Public Affairs & Corporate Communications. August 2014.

more about a healthy work-life balance than their parent's and grandparents' generations. These twenty-something employees won't likely be willing to overwork because their personal life is more of a priority than their work life. In fact, one of the rewards they are working for is to be able to work *less*—not more. Keep this in mind before setting an example that workaholism is the way to the rewards—because they will not respond well to such an example.

Provide Ample Training

A leader wears many hats. One of the most important is providing personal and professional development to the team. Gone are the days of big in-house training departments. Today, training and development has gone almost entirely virtual. This should be great—it means that your team has instant access to resources that will help them grow their business.

However, salespeople are pulled in so many directions that training and development are easily categorized as back-burner activities reserved for when they have some extra time. But who has extra time? The level of personal and professional development you pursue is in direct correlation with the amount of money and other rewards you earn. By providing your team with ongoing training and encouraging them to pursue personal development, you'll be helping them to earn more money and greater rewards. You'll also be showing them you care and want to see them succeed.

Have Their Backs

Your team wants to know you'll go to bat for them. You have to be an ally, not a boss. There are several ways to show your team that you have their backs. For starters, make sure they are aware you empathize with them. Think back to the days when you were a salesperson and treat your team the way you would have wanted to be treated. Putting yourself in your employees' shoes will go a long way to showing you support them. It's also important to explicitly tell your people you have their backs. You may think they know, but often times the opposite is true. Find ways to tell them. Just as important as telling them you have their backs is showing them you have their backs, so make sure your actions are true to your words.

If a client calls with a problem and blames your rep, give him or her the opportunity to explain what happened from their perspective. Let them know you support them and will diffuse the situation with the client. Or if a rep is having a bad day, doesn't feel well, or is going through issues at home, be kind and supportive, and encourage them to shut down, regroup, and come back tomorrow refreshed.

Lighten Up

Create an environment where your employees actually enjoy talking with you. I remember days when I would literally feel anxiety prior to every one-on-one call I had with my boss. The calls were a fire squad session of questions drilling me, no conversation, very micromanagy, always serious, and never light. Give your team a break. Be someone they want to speak with not someone who brings anxiety and ill feelings. Your team must feel that they are free to talk to you when they need your help and guidance. Listen openly and be encouraging. If they have issues, help resolve them. Your team should feel that they can come to you and be open and honest, while allowing you to be the same with them. Lightening up will go a long way to helping them do this.

Let Salespeople Do It Their Way

People have their own unique style and manner through which they best operate. Part of creating a positive work environment is allowing each person to do what works for him or her. If they get the right results and the rewards they are after doing it their way, feel comfortable loosening the reins. No two salespeople are the same and there is no one right selling style for getting top results. What works for one doesn't always work for the other, so be sure to encourage behaviors and selling styles that work for each individual.

ENCOURAGE HEALTHY COMPETITION

Contests are a great way to drive performance, increase engagement, make work more fun, and reward team members for a job well done. Salespeople are naturally competitive and this drive to outperform colleagues can be a powerful motivator. In fact, according to one study, competition with other team members was second only to recognition as a non-cash incentive to improve performance.[6]

But to be effective, contests must be set up properly. Here are a few tips to keep in mind when designing contests for your team.

Structure contests around business objectives

The most effective sales contests (those that have the most benefit for both your team and your company) are designed to achieve a specific business objective. So when creating contests, ask yourself what it is you want to accomplish. Some examples include:

- Increasing client appointments
- Obtaining new customers
- Achieving sales targets by month end
- Securing the largest order/contract
- Securing new client testimonials
- Selling special inventory or packages
- Ramping up sales of new products
- Improving sales performance

Once you've settled on your objective, create a contest that encourages and rewards behavior that helps accomplish that objective. For example, if you want to improve sales performance, you could have a contest that challenges salespeople to

6 Peter Ostrow, "Motivate, Incent, Compensate, Enable: Sales Performance Management Best Practices" (Aberdeen Group, 2013), 12.

exceed their numbers for the previous week, month, or quarter.

Simple is better

Don't overcomplicate sales contests. Make them easy to track. It can be very tempting to try to motivate everything that's important to making sales. The problem is, if you have too much happening, your team may get confused. A better approach is to have contests that concentrate on one or two behaviors that will move the needle most.

Keep them short

When sales contests go on too long, salespeople get bored with them, reducing their effectiveness. Take advantage of salespeople's natural sense of urgency by running contests in short bursts. This will help keep your team rallied and focused. Try running month-long, or even week-long contests to keep interest and motivation high.

Give away multiple, tiered awards

One problem I've seen with many sales contests is that superstars are the ones who usually win them. So, who do they really motivate besides the people who are already motivated? To make contests more interesting and appealing, award those who finish in second, third, and fourth place as well as first place. This will increase employee engagement by allowing more members of your team to enjoy the benefits of the contest.

Make sure everyone has a chance to win

The best contests give everyone an equal opportunity to take home a prize. One way to do this is to have salespeople compete against themselves. For example, you could set up a contest that rewards team members who had the greatest increase in sales, based on percentage. That way a newbie salesperson can compete with a seasoned pro.

Go beyond revenue

If you base your contests solely on revenue, chances are the same people, your Top Performers, will win every time. Instead, think about what you would like your team members to do more efficiently then create contests that reward them for behaviors that accomplish that goal. When choosing award categories, be sure to focus on behaviors that drive sales. For example you could reward team members for:

- Most new appointments scheduled
- Most new opportunities added to the pipeline
- Most referrals and introductions received
- Most new accounts or customers
- Most new sales (number of new sales closed, not revenue)
- Biggest new opportunity added to the pipeline or closed
- Most deals closed within a specific timeframe

By following this contest format, you'll not only enable more team members to be winners, you'll also be training them to be better salespeople.

Award prizes instead of cash

In my experience, the cash rewards of most sales contests are so little that they really don't impress reasonably well-paid salespeople. A better approach is to offer prizes. A study done by Goodyear Tires revealed that prizes can drive as much as forty-six percent higher performance than cash awards.[7] Some ideas for prizes you can offer include:

- Merchandise—Better than a cash prize because it is more permanent evidence of achievement. An added bonus: You can often get merchandise to use as prizes through donations from vendors, trade deals or at wholesale prices, enabling you to give larger prizes than if cash were used.
- Travel—The status, prestige, glamour, and fun associated with an exotic or exciting trip makes travel a popular prize. Plus, trips can include spouses and partners, which helps get them involved and in the right frame of mind to support the extra effort it takes to win contests.

7 Mike Martin, "Enhance the Impact of Contests Through Prizes Instead of Cash," Sales Compensation Focus (blog), World at Work, March 2013, https://www.worldatwork.org/adimComment?id=71593

- Special Privileges—Try offering a special dinner or lunch, extra vacation days, a reserved parking spot, or other special privileges as prizes.

Sales contests can be fun, motivating, and help build team spirit. When designed to accomplish a few clear, realistic objectives, they can also reinforce company values and good selling principles. All of which makes contests an invaluable tool for both driving top performance and rewarding employees for a job well done.

HAVE SOME SERIOUS FUN

I've had some jobs during my career that were total snooze fests. I've also worked in a few places where we had a blast—the kinds of workplaces I actually looked forward to going to each day. At one of my former companies, sponsors paid for us to go to lunch at the most exclusive restaurants, fly by helicopter to a small nearby island, go on boat rides in the Pacific Ocean. I would schedule team meetings at the beach. Yes, we actually got to sit on beach chairs and talk business. When business was done we shut off our phones and bonded. We learned more about one another on a personal level and it made us stronger.

When I started leading my own teams, I tried to make sure *fun* was always on the weekly agenda. Not everyone always got along, but I expected that and never forced the issue. When we were out having fun, I also used that time to give recognition to the team. Allowing and even encouraging your team to let loose a little shows that you see them as more than work drones, that you hear and understand their issues, and that you are willing to help them through it all—and have a little fun in the process.

Your people need to feel seen, heard, and appreciated by you, in the sense that they know you only want what's best for them—and having fun plays a big part in promoting that feeling.

Just as it is with anything in life, having fun at work requires balance. I once worked with a peer who everyone loved because he was able to lighten up the most serious conversations. It was fabulous—until it became excessive. He always cracked jokes, but his timing was often poor and inappropriate. Conversely, I worked with someone who was ultra serious and our weekly one-on-one's were dreadfully somber. Even if I tried to lighten up the conversation, my leader would default to a serious mode. I experienced stress and anxiety every time I knew we had to talk. Avoid these types of traits and find a balance, and your team will reap more of the rewards they desire.

Being intense all the time won't work, but being the kind of boss that no one takes seriously because you're always joking around isn't the right choice either. Find a balance between the two, and you'll soon discover that work is more enjoyable, not just for your team, but for you as well.

Choose to take the Fun Freeway to work each day.

Your team will be glad you do and they will be more likely to take the same road to work. Putting fun into your day increases performance because your team is excited to get up and sell. Find ways you can have fun that benefit your team.

It is not enjoyable to work in a chronically serious working environment. That means it's up to you to keep that fun meter of yours at a respectable level. Have some fun and lighten up when appropriate. Laugh. Change things up. Find ways to make serious subjects, calls, and meetings fun, light, and exciting. The response will be much better. Richard Branson said it best when he said:

"80% of your life is spent working. You want to have fun at home. Why shouldn't you have fun at work?"

The world of sales and sales management is loaded with enough stress and pressure. Why not find more fun at work? When people know things are not always going to be somber and serious, they will enjoy their job more. When your team is happy, they will not mind, and may even look forward to, coming to and participating in weekly meetings, calls, and one-on-ones. They will also want to keep working with a team who knows how to make work fun, which will reduce turnover.

My father taught me to always be humble. Even though I had to say goodbye to him at such an early age, his lessons remained with me. I knew not to steal the spotlight from my team and to never use anyone else's successes to self-promote. I wanted to be known for producing results, not for inflating my ego.

People work because they want something. They aren't working to help you retire early. They are working for a bigger paycheck, for their own retirement, for their children's future, for recognition, and for a sense of purpose. Help them achieve everything they want in a positive, fun environment, and you will become the kind of Elite sales leader that your Top Performing team deserves and loves working with.

IT'S YOUR TURN

Your team is working hard for the money. They're also working for the recognition they deserve. So, don't be shy. Give thanks out freely! Top Performers may be self-motivated, but even the best of the best crave rewards and recognition. Here are some questions to assess how much recognition and fun are a part of your management style:

Does each employee understand how to maximize the compensation plan to earn the highest financial incentives available?

____

____

____

Do you know what rewards motivate each of your employees?

____

____

____

Based on what you just read, what is one new reward – monetary or non-monetary—that you can start using to motivate Low Performers? Average Performers? Top Performers?

____

____

____

Think of the last time you mediated a conflict between one of your salespeople and a client. Did you hear both sides, or did you side with the client by default? If you sided with the client without hearing both sides out, how did your salesperson react?

____

____

____

Do you have a formal recognition system in place? If so, what types of accomplishments do you regularly recognize?

____

____

____

Which of your salespeople do you recognize the most? Do you think you spotlight the same ones too often or not enough?

____

____

____

What was the last fun activity you planned for your team as a group? Did everyone attend? Was it actually fun for them?

____

____

____

What kinds of fun activities can you plan in the future? Ask your team for their input and ideas.

____

____

____

CLOSING THOUGHTS

TIMES HAVE CHANGED, so our management techniques need to change with them. In today's world of sales management, the outdated techniques of days gone by aren't working anymore—and now I hope you see why. If you want to rise to the top to be with the best of the best, the Elite, you can use these principles to achieve your own success. You aren't interested in fluffy principles; you want proven techniques that drive results. Well, ask and you shall receive. These have proven to work for me and they can for you, too. Remember, Top Performers always duplicate their efforts.

I want to hear your stories and your successes. What did you try that worked? How can I help you? I would also love to discuss the possibility of working with you individually or with your company. I will enjoy getting you know you and your team in our future encounters and maybe even work together to help push your sales team to the top—and then stay there.

Thanks for reading my book.
I'll see you at the top of the ranking report.

MORE ABOUT DIANE

DIANE HAS HAD a long and successful career managing sales teams in the corporate world. For the majority of her twenty-plus years in corporate sales and sales management, she has consistently ranked at the top amongst her peers and top in nationwide rankings year after year. Diane's experience spans from working with small start-ups to large Fortune 100 clients such as Sony, Fox, Toyota, Tenet Healthcare, Universal Studios, and many more.

Diane has consistently excelled through multiple corporate reorganizations, mergers, tremendous turnover, and having to report to a variety of mangers, directors, and top executives. Diane attributes her success to her unwavering drive and motivation, along with her ability to bring heart and fun to the corporate working environment.

Diane worked for Sprint for nearly fourteen years, where she led one of the top-performing teams nationwide year after year, allowing her to achieve multiple Presidents' Club Awards, as well as leading some of her direct Account Managers to achieve multiple Presidents' Club Awards. She also created and pioneered a new National Accounts division and successfully created new ways to realign team territories and account assignments.

She then moved to American Express to become the Director of Business Development. Along with this position, she inherited a team ranked #33 in the nation. In less than two years, she led her team to become the #10 ranking team nationwide, and onward to become #4 nationwide in January of her third year with the company.

Diane grew up in the suburbs of Chicago. She holds two degrees, a B.S. in Management and a M.A. in Spiritual Psychology. She has traveled to more than fifteen European countries. In addition to traveling, she also enjoys volunteering, music, cooking, golf, and advocating for children.

While other experts share theory-based principles and techniques, Diane's tell-it-like-it-is style is refreshing, fun, and highly effective for today's business environment. Her *reality-based principles* are easy for any corporation to understand and implement to get FAST results. She's highly intuitive and has an amazing talent for getting to the bottom line FAST.

Want to learn what it takes to stand out in the corporate world?

The Solution is Simple.

Diane Polnow will show you what it takes to get to the top of the ranking report FAST

... and then stay there!

I'D LIKE TO HEAR FROM YOU

How did you climb to the top using
my proven techniques?

What principles did you use that
improved your teams results?

What challenges are you facing that you'd like help with?

Share your success stories and ask top questions on my Facebook and Twitter pages.

Hire Diane For:
Consulting
Coaching
Training
Keynote Speaker

For inquiries to Consult, Coach, Train, or Speak please contact:

www.EliteSalesLeaders.com
www.DianePolnow.com
Phone: 310.421.5271